the Project Success Checklist

Drive Alignment, **Produce** Results, *and*
Reduce the Risk of Project Failure

Roger Kastner

Simple Frameworks
Publishing

SIMPLE FRAMEWORKS PUBLISHING

the PROJECT SUCCESS CHECKLIST

Drive Alignment, Produce Results, and Reduce the Risk of
Project Failures

Roger Kastner

Copyediting by Karissa Lagos
Cover and interior design by Tabitha Lahr
Front cover photo © istockphoto.com
Back cover author photo © Duncan McDougall/Slalom, LLC

Published in the United States by SIMPLE FRAMEWORKS PUBLISHING
ISBN: 978-0-9863430-0-1

To Lara, Duncan, and Ian,

*I cannot imagine being more loved, more inspired,
or more grateful for you three.*

Contents

Section 3—Making Your Own Project Success Checklist

SECTION 1

Project Success Checklist

Introduction

Several years ago, I was working for a start-up web company and found myself enjoying a moment of relaxation. We had launched our new product that was going to bring our company back from the brink of extinction, and it was my project that I had just successfully managed to completion that was the point of our group celebration. The president had a few nice words to say, gave a toast, and then she walked straight up to me.

Being young and naïve, I thought I was going to be the recipient of a high five or an impromptu week vacation, but instead I received what felt like more of an interrogation.

"Why was this project successful?" she said poignantly.

Without a better answer, I went for humor. "The stars must have been aligned." It was a good question and I honestly had not thought about it. The president did not find my answer amusing; in fact, she was insistent. "No, you did something different on this project," she told me, "and I want you to figure that out and let us know so we can repeat it."

There I was, beer in one hand, sporting a Hawaiian shirt, (it was the 90s), completely dumbstruck. Not only was I unable answer to a simple question, "What made this project successful?" but somehow I just launched one of the first successful projects and I could not even get through the launch party without being assigned my next task.

Unfortunately, that task took slightly longer than the company did; however, it did teach me that project success is not something that should be left to fate or astrology.

Now, as most project managers can attest, project failures are easy to spot. There are many obvious signs of project failure, and if the research studies holds true, you have likely witnessed several of these symptoms before: a lot of late-night and early-morning meetings; shouting behind closed conference room doors; e-mails written in ALL CAPS; coworkers spending a lot of time on LinkedIn. If you were to ask anyone on the failed project why it failed, they would instantly be able to identify a reason or two—and regardless of accuracy, those opinions are usually pretty strong.

In contrast, when a project succeeds, it is much more difficult to identify the two or three factors that contributed to its success. If you asked the team members involved in a successful project what contributed to their success, their answers would likely be a little less clear and their tone less sure. That's because project success doesn't happen when just a few things come together, but rather, success happens when a *series* of contributing factors occur on a project.

In the ensuing years after my discussion with the president who started me down the path to discover the secret sauce of project success, I've also learned the importance of how we define "success" itself. The common definition of project success is delivering a project on scope, on schedule, and on budget—and yet to me that feels more like project *survival* than success. Organizations fund projects to achieve a positive outcome, and that outcome is expected to be multiples of the project investment. And yes, delivering a project on scope, on schedule, and on budget will result in the successful management of the investment, but it doesn't necessarily produce the ultimate goal of creating that positive outcome, also known as the "R" in the Return on Investment. No, project success should be more than just managing the investment; it should be about the impact of the project.

For all the talk about project success, however, its occurrence might be less common than you might expect. Depending on the industry, research studies peg project success rates between 30% and 70%—from well below a failing grade to a C-minus. I will presume that you and I share a desire to perform at a higher level, and therefore, wouldn't you do whatever you could to increase the likelihood of success? I would too, and my search for an answer to the question of what led to the success of that project early in my career has led me to a powerful tool: the checklist.

> "Dr. Atul Gawande, Captain Sullenberger, and Moses walk into a bar. The bartender looks up and says, 'Hey, is this a joke?'"

Dr. Atul Gawande, Captain Sullenberger, and Moses are famous figures for many reasons, and one of those reasons is their use of lists.

Dr. Gawande's best-selling book *The Checklist Manifesto* highlights the value of checklists as a significant contributing factor to ensuring better outcomes in the operating room, and he goes on to cite many examples elsewhere where lists contribute to success.

You may recall the story of US Airways Flight 1459: In January 2009, Captain Sullenberger and First Officer Jeffrey Skiles successfully averted catastrophe when they landed their airplane in the Hudson River after losing engine power. While Captain Sullenberger was making the decision to attempt a water landing in the Hudson River, First Officer Jeffrey Skiles was following a checklist in attempt to restart the engines. Once Captain Sullenberger determined where they were going, First Officer Skiles used another checklist to prepare the cabin for a water landing. Through these efforts, they saved themselves and their passengers.

And Moses, well, as the story goes, he had more than a little guidance in making his list of Ten Commandments, but he ended up with what might be the most famous list of them all.

What follows may not be as important as brain surgery, safe air travel, or rules to live by, but the process outlined in this book can provide value in your daily professional life and lead to increasing the likelihood of success on your projects. Who knows, your future projects may have significant and long-lasting impacts on your immediate community or even the greater world.

The Project Success Checklist captures the process I have developed for creating, using, and improving a checklist of factors that contribute to project success. I have been developing and refining this process for almost a decade with positive results; with your help, I hope, it will continue to be employed and enhanced for a long time.

Originally developed as a workshop to help my coworkers identify contributing factors that result in successful projects, I've shared the process for creating a Project Success Checklist with client and industry audiences for the last five years. During that time I have also written a blog series about the Project Success Checklist process entitled *Why Projects Succeed* series for the Slalom Consulting Blog.[1] It's because of that experience, and because of the encouragement I've received from my readers and audiences, that I've now written about the process *as* a book. I hope you enjoy it.

My intention in writing this book is to share with you a simple process and tool I have found that helps me focus on the critical things that drive successful projects. In this book, I'll share with you:

- Why a Project Success Checklist is valuable

- How I first came across a project success list

---

1. The Slalom Consulting Blog showcases the thoughts and work of talented consultants. Slalom Consulting is a growing business and technology consulting firm. To learn more, go to: http://www.slalom.com

- How to define success for your projects

- How to measure a project manager's contribution toward a project's success

- My Project Success Checklist

- Some humorous stories from my attempts to learn and apply success factors

- How to develop your own Project Success Checklist

- How to use your Project Success Checklist with sponsors and stakeholders

- Why a Project Success Checklist by itself is not enough to ensure success

I hope you find much value in this book and in using the process for developing a Project Success Checklist. I wish you good luck on your projects, because if the industry research on project success rates are even close to being accurate, a little luck wouldn't hurt to go along with our disciplined approach to producing successful project results.

CHAPTER 1

Why a Checklist for Success

Why do I need a Checklist for Success?

Checklists are not new to Project Management. Checklists exist for project chartering, scheduled development, requirements gathering, and on and on. There are so many Project Management checklists for the minute details of projects that I'm sure there are even checklists for project checklists somewhere out there. However, that is not what this is all about. The checklist I'm talking about is a Project Success Checklist—one that captures the factors that make or break a project. So, why do we need a Checklist for Success? Allow me to break that question into two parts:

1. Do project managers need help in achieving project success?

2. Why would a checklist be the right answer for how to achieve project success?

Do project managers need help in achieving success?

The first thing you should know about me is that I'm a consultant. Similar to lawyers and doctors, a consultant's answer to many questions is, "It depends." If you are a project manager whose projects are successful each and every time, I'd like to first shake your hand and then suggest that you pass your copy of this book along to someone whose success rate is not as remarkable. However, before we do all that, let's first make sure we have the same definition of success.

I do not accept the standard definition of success as delivering the project on scope, on schedule, and on budget. Yes, those are valuable pieces of the success puzzle; however, I believe there is more to the project success equation. Let me provide two of my past projects as examples and then let you decide which one was a success.

The first project had an on-scope, on-schedule, and on-budget delivery, but the product completely flopped in the marketplace. In hindsight, it was apparent that we were really, really good at building the wrong thing. There was no return on investment (ROI) at all.

On the second project, the scope, schedule, and budget were blown out of the water by mid-project. The end product we delivered, however, was a huge success for the company as deemed by users, stakeholders, and our sponsor, meeting all expectations and ROI objectives.

So, considering the above two projects, which one would you call "successful"?

I believe the definition of project success should include more than simply being on scope, on schedule, and on budget—that it should also encompass appropriately setting, managing, and delivering on your sponsor's expectations for a product or result that produces the promised ROI. Organizations approve and fund projects with the promise of an ROI; being on schedule and on budget is crucial in the management of the "I," and may sometimes impact the "R," so those are definitely yardsticks against which to measure success. However, that original approval decision was based on the "R." And when it comes to the "R," even if we accept project success as referring to being on scope, on schedule, and on budget, our discipline does not have a great track record there. Let's look at the data to see where project success rates come in.

Depending on which study you want to believe, the success rate for projects is between 30% and 70%. The Standish Group researches and produces reports on IT projects' success rates as measured upon original estimates of scope, schedule, and budget. The 2013 report found that only 39% of IT projects achieved an on-scope, on-schedule, and on-budget delivery, with 43% of projects identified as "challenged" (over budget or late), and 18% cancelled or never implemented.[2] Another IT project success rate study, this one performed by *Dr. Dobb's Journal* in 2010,[3] asked participants to rate success based on the identified success criteria of their projects rather than by the "on-schedule and on-budget" definition. The *Dr. Dobb's* numbers are a little more encouraging than The Standish Group's but probably lower than most project managers and their sponsors would consider acceptable:

- Ad-hoc projects: 49% are successful, 37% are challenged, and 14% are failures

- Iterative projects: 61% are successful, 28% are challenged, and 11% are failures

- Agile projects: 60% are successful, 28% are challenged, and 12% are failures

- Traditional projects: 47% are successful, 36% are challenged, and 17% are failures

2. The Standish Group is an IT research and consulting firm in Massachusetts that periodically publishes the results of their surveys. The *CHAOS Report* provides IT project success rates, and over the years has shown success rates staying roughly the same, in the thirties. Their method of measuring project success based on original estimates is somewhat controversial due to the fact that this definition does not account for approved changes to scope, schedule, and budget baselines, while the Scope Change Management process for approving changes to baselines is an accepted standard process within the Project Management discipline. For more information, go to: http://www.standishgroup.com

3. Dr. Dobb's 2010 IT Project Success Rates report was based on findings from three surveys, so participants were self-selected and this was not as an exhaustive study as The Standish Group's study. That said, it is good to see the increase in success rates. For more information on the report, please go to: http://www.drdobbs.com/architecture-and-design/2010-it-project-success-rates/226500046

Okay, let's look beyond IT project success rates; hopefully those numbers are better, right?

LARGE CONSTRUCTION

In 2009, an ominously titled report, *Delusion and Deception in Large Infrastructure Projects*, [4] cited a study that looked at 250 mega-construction projects in over twenty counties and found that nine out of ten had significant cost overruns.

BUSINESS PROCESS OUTSOURCING

The *Offshore 2005 Research: Preliminary Findings and Conclusions*[5] report by the Ventoro organization in 2005 found that 55% of outsourcing projects failed to achieve their objectives. Additionally, a survey of CIOs conducted by Harvey Nash found that 79% of respondents said their outsourcing projects had met or exceeded their *expectations*, but only 18% indicated that their outsourcing projects had met all *objectives*.[6] The split between objectives and expectations raises some interesting questions. For example: Did 61% of CIOs have low expectations for their outsourcing projects, or was it that their objectives were too unrealistic?

PUBLIC SECTOR

At a 2010 Department of Energy Project Management conference, researchers presented their findings that over a three-year span, 74% of projects were delivered according to specification and within 10% of original cost baseline. Diving deeper into the numbers, they reported that projects with less than $50M budgets had an 83% success rate, whereas for projects with budgets greater than $750M, the success rates dropped to 40%.[7]

---

4. I laugh every time I read that title. The main point of the *Delusion & Deception in Large Infrastructure Projects* study is not that these mega-projects are typically over budget and late by significant amounts, but that "either project leaders are delusionally optimistic or lying to [the] public" about cost and schedule estimates. The study was produced by Bent Flyvbjerg (Professor, Aalborg University), Massimo Garbuio (Lecturer, University of Sydney), and Dan Lovallo (Professor, University of Sydney, and Fellow, University of California at Berkeley).

5. 55% of outsourcing projects fail to meet objectives—wow! Offshore 2005 Research: Preliminary Findings and Conclusions, Ventoro, 2005: www.ventoro.com

6. Harvey Nash, 2007/2008 CIO Survey, 2008: www.harveynash.com/usa

7. Department of Energy Project Management Workshop presentation delivered by Paul Bosco. For more information, go to: http://energy.gov/sites/prod/files/maprod/documents/01_Bosco_Get_Off_GAO_High_Risk_List.pdf

CHANGE MANAGEMENT

IBM's two-year study of 1,500 change practitioners, the 2008 *Global Making Change Work*,[8] found that only 41% of change initiatives were deemed successful relative to time, cost, and quality objectives. When PricewaterhouseCoopers published their 2012 report looking at project success rates from thirty-four different industries across thirty-eight countries, meanwhile, they found that 70% of projects achieved their scope, schedule, and budget objectives.[9]

So, depending on which study you want to hang your hat on, project success is somewhere between 30% and 70%, which is, as I said earlier, somewhere between a C-minus and abysmal.

Maybe success does not come easily for most project managers most of the time. And if you are like me, then I'm sure you will take any bit of help to increase the likelihood of success on your projects. Now to address our second question: Why would a checklist help increase the likelihood of project success?

WHY A CHECKLIST?

Ever since Dr. Atul Gawande's *The Checklist Manifesto* hit the bookshelves, the world of lists hasn't been the same. Dr. Gawande's book details how prevalent checklists are in the operating room, as well as in the business world, to help ensure successful outcomes. This observation came as a big surprise to him.

Early in his book, Dr. Gawande highlights how his colleagues were able to reduce the rates of errors in surgery as well as post-operation complications by the use of checklists at Johns Hopkins. More surprising was what the checklists contained: simple reminders. Not instructions on how to do the complicated procedures or problem solving, but instead the type of stuff he thought as surgeons, those highly educated and talented professionals, would consider to be the "stupid stuff."

---

8. The full IBM Global Making Change Work study can be found here: http://www-935.ibm.com/services/us/gbs/bus/pdf/gbe03100-usen-03-making-change-work.pdf

9. PricewaterhouseCoopers 2012 study The Insights and Trends: Current Portfolio, Programme, and Project Management Practices is available here: http://www.pwc.com/en_US/us/public-sector/assets/pwc-global-project-management-report-2012.pdf

Surgeons have a reputation as being confident, self-assured, and cava-lier. Having a firsthand familiarity with this reputation, Dr. Gawande was taken aback by the presence, let alone use, of checklists in the operating room. Additionally, since the checklists were now a standard procedure, others in the operating room such as nurses or assisting physicians felt empowered to reinforce the adherence to the checklist whereas in the past they might not have due to the power dynamic in the room. The check-list proved to be effective in reducing the power-distance between profes-sionals, which has prevented subordinates from speaking up in the past, whether in the operating room or cockpit in many documented failures.

Dr. Gawande borrowed the checklist findings from his colleagues at Johns Hopkins and applied it to a project he was working on with the World Health Organization which came to be known as the Safe Sur-gery Checklist. After its first implementation in eight hospitals, the Safe Surgery Checklist was found to reduce major complications by 30%, deaths by 47%, and infections by half.[10] Though his research and experi-ence, Dr. Gawande created his theory of checklists: "Under conditions of complexity, not only are checklists a help, they are required for suc-cess. There must always be room for judgment, but judgment aided and even enhanced by procedure."[11] While researching the use of checklists in other professions and see if the results at Johns Hopkins was unique to healthcare, Dr. Gawande looked at examples from construction, the restaurants, and in logistics, and found the best source for not only us-ing checklists but creating checklists is the cockpit.

The next time you board a flight, look into the cockpit and you will likely see two very intelligent, highly trained, and experienced profes-sionals reviewing laminated cards, flipping through books, or shuffling route maps. The pilot's pre-flight routine includes going over multiple checklists to ensure the aircraft is ready to fly. The checklist review pro-cess repeats throughout the flight and on the ground afterward, during the process of landing, and finally parking at the gate.

---

10. *The Checklist Manifesto*, Dr. Atul Gawande, pg. 154
11. Ibid, pg. 79

Several years ago I went down to a municipal airport and hired a flight instructor for a sixty-minute flight.[12] The flight instructor walked me to a Cessna 152, which looked like a typical private aircraft except that it was really, really small. This plane was so small and cramped, it was as if we had to alternate our inhalations when sitting next to each other in the cockpit for lack of room for us to breathe in at the same time.

When we first walked over to the plane, the instructor started talking about various external parts of the aircraft, checking them for malfunctions as we went and making notations on a clipboard. At one point I looked at my watch, suspicious that he was trying to save money on fuel costs by taking a long time to explain why it was so important we had "the right mixture of oil to gas" and so on. He noticed, smiled, and said, "Don't worry, you're paying for air time, not ground time." Reassured, I went back to listening to him.

Once we made it inside the cockpit, we started going over all the other items on the checklist. It wasn't until a good fifteen to twenty minutes after reaching the airplane that we were actually ready for takeoff.

The use of checklists helps surgeons and pilots increase the likelihood of success by making sure they don't forget the simple stuff. The checklist ensures the coverage of the mundane, so the professional can focus on the hard problem-solving and process-intensive computations they are used to performing.

---

12. This was a tremendous amount of fun, or so it seems now. I, like a lot of people, don't like turbulence, and after a couple of bumpy flights, I was unsure if I ever wanted to get on a plane again. So on the advice of a friend, I went to the Palo Alto Municipal airport to learn more about flying and how turbulence works. Of course, the flight instructor there told me the best way to learn about flying and turbulence is not on the ground but instead in the air. My flight instructor, maybe twenty-five years old, asked if he could finish his burger and fries first, and I was only happy to have him complete his lunch as I was about to lose mine with the thought of what I was about to do. After the pre-flight checks and taxiing, we were pointed down the runway and my flight instructor told me to ease off the brakes, pull the throttle, and, when we hit 60 knots, pull the stick back 30 degrees. Within a couple minutes we were at 1,500 feet doing circles around Stanford University, watching 747s fly a couple thousand feet overhead. The flight instructor had his hands near the stick the whole time, but for the most part, she was my aircraft. When it was time to head in, we flew southbound, following the 101, made a U-turn when we were parallel with the Shoreline Amphitheater, and lined up with the runway—and that's when the my flight instructor told me to not touch the stick again until after we were safely on the ground, a command I gladly obeyed. My heart rate still increases when we hit bumps at 35,000 feet, but when that happens now I am reminded of the afternoon I spent sitting cheek to cheek with my flight instructor, having the flight of my life.

Simplistically speaking, relying on checklists to cover routine procedures is very similar to how our brains function. The basal ganglia in the brain stores our learned habits and procedures that are called upon and performed as needed.[13] For instance, when was the last time you had to think about brushing your teeth? It's probably been a long time since you were consciously thinking about slathering some toothpaste on your toothbrush and brushing your teeth. Instead you spend the next minute or two thinking about the events of the day or pretending you're a singer in a rock band (c'mon, you know you do it too).

It's in our prefrontal cortex where the big thinking—like deciding which song you will sing when you're palming that Sonicare in front of the mirror —happens. When new information comes into the brain via our senses, it first goes through the basal ganglia, where our brain determines if the information is mapped to a habit response. If so, we start our routine. If the new information is not mapped to a habit, the information is routed to our prefrontal cortex for some serious cogitation. According to Dr. David Rock's book *Your Brain at Work*, the prefrontal cortex uses a tremendous amount of energy while at work, so the brain purposely assigns new information to a habit as an efficiency and energy-saving technique.[14] This is an important point. I'm sure you have noticed that you are more likely to make a mistake when you are—or, more precisely, your brain is—tired. More on this in a moment.

As we were discussing before, Dr. Gawande found that surgeons and other professionals often made mistakes while performing routine procedures. The habit procedures imprinted in their basal ganglia failed at seemingly non-critical times, when they were used to being on *autopilot*. The checklist, then—both for surgical teams as well as for pilots

---

13. *The Power of Habit* is a wonderful book by Charles Duhigg that breaks down and maps the habit process and how to reengineer it. Fascinating stuff.

14. Dr. David Rock is *the* guy when it comes to neuroleadership—in fact, he coined the phrase. *Your Brain at Work* is a very informative and easy read, mixing up brain science with business logic and human interactions in a very consumable way. I highly recommend this book, it's one of my favorites.

in the cockpit—has proven to be a good "routine process" tool for professionals, increasing their likelihood of success and preventing simple mistakes when the habits imprinted in the limbic system might fail, especially if they are tired or under stress.

Let's return to Captain Sullenberger and First Officer Skiles so we can take a closer look at how their successful use of checklists helped them prevent a major catastrophe over the skies of New York City.

CASE STUDY: FLIGHT 1549

On January 15, 2009, US Airways Flight 1549 took off from La Guardia Airport in New York City for a routine flight to Charlotte, North Carolina—but soon after takeoff the Airbus 320 ran into a flock of geese at 3,200 feet, which resulted in the complete disabling of both engines. For Captain Chesley "Sully" Sullenberger, First Officer Jeffrey Skiles, and the 153 other people on the plane, the flight had suddenly become anything but routine.

One of the first things you hear on the black box recording after the bird strike is Captain Sullenberger requesting control of the aircraft. First Officer Skiles had been flying the aircraft—his hands had been on the stick—for takeoff, so with the words, "My aircraft," Captain Sullenberger requested that he be given control of plane. He did so not because he was more senior or had many more hours of flight time in the Airbus 320, which was the case, but because he knew Skiles had just completed certification training for the Airbus 320, which meant the first officer would be more likely to remember where the applicable checklists were in the flight manual.[15]

After running through the options and then deciding to attempt a water landing, Captain Sullenberger maneuvered to put the plane down near a busy ferry crossing so they would be closer to boats who could perform a rescue. While he was lining up the attempt, First Officer Skiles was using a checklist to perform the necessary steps to prepare the aircraft for a water landing.

---

15. Captain Chesley Sullenberger's and First Officer Jeffrey Skiles' heroics on Flight 1549 were truly inspirational for many, and have continued to be of great interest to me. I thoroughly enjoyed Sullenberger's autobiography, *Highest Duty: My Search for What Really Matters* as it tells his story of striving to be the best prepared, the best trained, and the most consistent pilot he could be. Tip of the hat to both Sully and Skiles; you sirs are made of the right stuff.

Remember the interplay between the basal ganglia's ability to perform routines and the prefrontal cortex's ability to process and problem-solve? By assigning First Officer Skiles the duties of restarting the engines and then preparing the aircraft for a water landing, Captain Sullenberger was doing what our brains do: compartmentalizing the work. He assigned the routine tasks (basal ganglia) to First Officer Skiles and the problem-solving tasks (prefrontal cortex) to himself.

While this next item might be considered nitpicking in the highest degree, it illustrates a point. The one step that First Officer Skiles missed on the "prepare for water landing" checklist was to flip a switch to seal the back end of the airplane, which caused the tail of the plane to sink below the water surface. Don't misunderstand me: With all passengers and crew alive and no one injured on the ground, I don't think anyone is going to fault First Officer Skiles. Truly, not a bad outcome for a passenger jet that lost both engines at 3,200 feet over the most densely populated area in the United States. But with only ninety seconds to complete the checklist while gliding towards the earth, can you imagine if Skiles *hadn't* had a checklist? According to Kitty Higgins, the National Transportation Safety Board's spokesperson, "This has to go down as the most successful ditching in aviation history. These people knew what they were supposed to do and they did it and as a result, nobody lost their life."[16]

Now let's be clear: Checklists are not the sole reason that Captain Sullenberger and First Officer Skiles successfully landed the plane in the Hudson River and consequently saved the lives of their passengers and crew. There were many contributing factors to the successful conclusion of Flight 1549. However, the use of the engine restart and water landing checklists after the bird strike, as well as Captain Sullenberger's reliance on First Officer Skiles' familiarity with those checklists, definitely contributed to the successful ditching of the plane in the Hudson River. First Officer Skiles' reliance on and ability to per-

---

16. *New York Post*, "Quiet Air Hero is Captain America," January 17, 2009

form the items on the relevant checklists in the minute and a half between the decision to ditch and the landing was critical to keeping the aircraft above the waterline long enough for ferry boats to reach the wingtips and rescue the stranded passengers. Ultimately, if it had not been for the skill and experience of both pilots, and their willingness to rely on their checklists, this story would likely have a far less amazing ending than it does.

The use of checklists to ensure the proper execution of normally routine patterns during a period of great stress highlights the value of the checklist. Both pilots had started engines thousands of times. Both pilots had trained on preparing an aircraft for a water landing. However, both pilots were also trained to rely on checklists to ensure the accurate completion of the steps required to perform the task at hand, and that— combined with the decision-making skills and physical talents of two dedicated pilots—helped to save the day.

Checklists alone are not the reason for successful results, of course: they are only reminders of what increases the likelihood of success. Dr. Gawande's theory about checklists needs to be repeated, "under the conditions of complexity, not only are checklists a help, they are required for success." In the end, it is the responsibility and skill of the professional who chooses to use the checklist that will lead to a successful outcome.

YOUR TURN

Now that I've answered the two questions, *Do project managers need help in achieving project success?* and *Why would a checklist be the right answer for how to achieve project success?*, how about you participate in the following activity and then answer a few questions for me? In honor of Captain Sullenberger's and First Officer Skiles' achievement, take the next seventy-three seconds and write down four to five factors that contribute to project success:

1) _____
_____
_____
_____

2) _____
_____
_____
_____

3) _____
_____
_____
_____

4) _____
_____
_____
_____

5) _____
_____
_____
_____

Time's up; pencils down. If you were creating your own Project Success Checklist, you'd be halfway done. Later in the book, I'll share all the steps you need to create and complete your own checklist.

Now I want to ask you three questions:

QUESTION #1: *Was it difficult to create a list of four to five project success factors?*

Probably not, because it only took a little over a minute to create your list. You might not think it's perfect yet, but I'm sure you wrote down a couple items that are good contributing factors for project success, so well done!

QUESTION #2: *Do you think it would be useful to have a list of prioritized success factors available to guide how you plan and manage your projects?*

If checklists are good enough to help surgeons reduce patient complications and for pilots to fly millions of flights safely each year, then they are probably a good idea for project managers, who also perform hundreds of routine tasks in order to complete their projects, too.

QUESTION #3: *Do you do this already?*

Well, if your answer to this question is "no," you are not alone. That's the most overwhelmingly common answer I receive time and time again when I ask this question. Regardless of how common-sense this practice is, it is not commonplace. Yet.

Now, of course project managers are familiar with checklists—some projects seeming to overflow with checklists for every procedure possible, in fact—but that is not the type of checklist I am proposing. I don't mean a checklist to ensure that the requirements gathering process is properly performed, or that the steps to build a use case are followed completely, or that user acceptance testing is conducted in adherence to an organization's quality standards. Nope, wrong checklist. The purpose of a Project Success Checklist is bigger than that; it aims to keep focus on the key factors that, if they're missing or not managed appropriately, will cause the project's likelihood of success to drop near zero—factors such as:

- *End user involvement*—proactively engaging target users or customers in defining the problem statement, reviewing and providing feedback on the new processes and designs, and reviewing the delivered end product prior to release.

- *Executive sponsorship*—visibly active and engaged in the project, making project decisions on recommendations, eliminating barriers to progress, and evangelizing the project amongst peers.

- *Clear business objectives*—well articulated, easy to understand, and quantifiable goals for the project which will be the basis for all project decisions and acceptance criteria.

Failing to identify these project factors poses a significant risk to the successful completion of a project. But when these factors are developed and focused upon, the likelihood for project success increases.

WHO NEEDS A PROJECT SUCCESS CHECKLIST?

About this time during my *Project Success Checklist* presentation, I usually catch a look of disbelief from an attendee or two that says, "Okay, Roger, I know that lists are good for some people, but I'm pretty detailed-oriented, and I know my stuff, so do I really need to write down a list of things I already know?" (Yes, a lot can be inferred from nonverbal cues). The answer is yes, but beyond the surgeon and the pilot and how they benefit from checklists, there are several other types of people who can benefit from the checklist:

- *Really smart people*—If surgeons and pilots—you know, the smartest-kid-in-the-class types—have found success by using checklists, then I'm sure they're beneficial for smart people in any profession. You may have heard someone say about a really experienced person, "She's forgotten more about the subject than I'll ever know." Well, the checklist is perfect for people who know so much about a subject that they may forget a mundane step that is crucial for success at a critical moment.

- *Really busy people*—You ever feel like you're going a thousand miles an hour, juggling several balls in the air, with so many e-mails in your inbox that you receive network administrator e-mails notifying you that you're about to exceed your size limit, and it's only 8:30 a.m.? Yes, I'm sure you do—and I'm sure you refer to those moments as "only days that end in a 'Y.'" Really busy people benefit from lists because they help them keep on track and not let anything slip between the cracks. In David Allen's book *Getting Things Done*, he suggests keeping a *single* to-do list, not many separate to-do lists (e.g., sticky notes on your monitor, your smartphone, and your whiteboard). A single list that's accessible to you from most places, he says, is a best practice for busy people who want to ensure they get *things* done (hence the title). The value of the single to-do list, Mr. Allen continues, is that it allows you to see everything on your list and then prioritize each item against all competing tasks. This is the idea behind the Project Success Checklist as well: it allows you to keep all the priority factors that contribute to project success in one place.

- *Big idea people*—Okay, these people might be called "daydreamers" or "pie-in-the-sky types," and they might be easily distracted by bright and shiny objects (admittedly, I can sometimes fall into this category). Lists, frameworks, cheat sheets, and crib notes are very useful for these types of people because with so many competing thoughts in their brain, along with the possibility that a new idea will come screaming into the party at any minute, having tools that help remind them of the correct steps in a process is crucial to 1) achieve repeatable successful outcomes, and 2) keep from forgetting something important.

- *People who lack experience*—Hats off to the person who understands that "strength is in the knowledge of one's weaknesses" and embraces lists and other aids to help them accomplish tasks and goals.

I'm sure there are other types of people who can benefit from making and using lists than those that fit into the above categories, however, it seems logical that if the smartest kid and the "dumbest" (or "least experienced") kid in the class and everyone in between can benefit from lists, you can too.

How did I come up with the idea for the Project Success Checklist? With a little help from my friends, of course. In the next chapter, I'll give you the history of the Project Success Checklist and how it fell into my lap.

KEY POINTS FOR CHAPTER 1:

- Project success rates, across many industries, need to improve. And if you are reading this book, you want to improve yours. The Project Success Checklist is a low-cost, high-reward approach for increasing the likelihood of project success.

- Checklists have been proven to be useful for highly intelligent, highly trained, and highly experienced professionals performing routine procedures who are more likely to forget something simple than something complex.

- Everyone can benefit from using checklists; so can you.

- Captain Sullenberger and First Officer Skiles are heroes.

CHAPTER 2

How I First Came to
Love the Checklist

In January 2005, I attended the Project Management Institute's *Seminar World* learning event in San Francisco, where I had the pleasure of attending a keynote speech by Jim Johnson, CEO of The Standish Group. As you may recall from the last chapter, The Standish Group is an IT research and consulting firm that produces studies on success rates for IT projects. Mr. Johnson's keynote was titled, "Top Ten Reasons Projects Succeed and the Five Reasons They Fail," and like most project managers, I was excited about learning anything I could that would help me lead more successful projects. At the time, The Standish Group had researched over 40,000 projects within a ten-year timeframe, so Mr. Johnson had quite a lot of data to back his story.

Mr. Johnson started his keynote with the five reasons why projects fail, and we in the audience laughed at the funny, yet sadly true points he made (as my wife often reminds me, there is a little bit of truth in every joke). The list was funny *precisely* because most in attendance had gone through painful experiences related to each failure factor Mr. Johnson announced. The five causes of project failure he cited were:

1. Ambition—failure to understand project/product limitations

2. Arrogance—failure to acknowledge what the team cannot produce

3. Ignorance—failure to understand what the team can do

4. Fraudulence—lying about team's capabilities

5. Abstinence—not paying enough attention to the project to ensure its success

As I said, this was a humorous and interesting list. Yet as a project manager, I struggled with the notion that I would not have much control over these factors. Sure, I might be able to validate concerns about overextending our team skills in the case of Arrogance, or provide awareness and recommendations on issues related to misunderstanding the capabilities of the technology in the case of Ambition—but I didn't feel like I could truly influence or effect change in any of the failure factors on the list. These belonged in the realm of senior leadership; they were more like warning signs for me to look out for than actionable items. I felt like if I were to discover that one or more of these failure factors were present on my project, my best course of action would be to polish the resume and start looking for another position.

Fortunately, Mr. Johnson offered us the flip side of the coin with The Standish Group's list of top ten reasons that projects succeed. I liked the success factor list a lot better than the failure list because these factors were clearly positives steps that I, as the project manager, could implement to increase the likelihood of my project's success.

Here are the factors that Mr. Johnson presented as the top ten reasons IT projects succeed:

- User Involvement

- Executive Management Support

- Clear Business Objectives

- Experienced Project Managers

- Minimized Scope and Requirements

- Agile

- Skilled Resources

- Formal Methodology

- Financial Management

- Standard Tools & Infrastructure

Now this was a list I could use. I immediately began to think about how I could apply these success factors to my projects. I could apply "User Involvement" by asking business stakeholders to identify a representative group of targeted users who could provide feedback on our prototypes instead of relying on the feedback from our team leads, as was our original plan. For "Executive Sponsorship," I could ensure that the next time I met with my sponsor I would approach the meeting from the perspective of "thinking how to best engage the sponsor" rather than it feeling like the conversation was a test of my knowledge and capabilities. That approach would force me to change my pre-meeting activities from studying project data, as if the meeting was a college midterm, to thinking about the role of the sponsor, identifying their needs and concerns, determining what the project needed from them, and presenting that back to them in the best way possible. As I continued down the list, I made notes of all the things I needed to do differently on my project. At the end of the keynote presentation, I was truly excited to get back to work and incorporate the success factors into my project.

When I got back to my office and started to incorporate the factors I'd learned about into my project plans and activities, I ran into a slight snag. In the excitement of the moment at the keynote presentation, I had not realized that three of the factors were not applicable in my company's environment:

1. "Agile"—more specifically, the Agile development methodology[17]—was not an accepted practice within the software team to which I was assigned, so that wasn't useful.

2. At that time in my company, a "formal methodology" did not exist. We were a 2,500-person technology company that was made up of several acquired start-ups and partnerships, spread across the globe, whose Project Management resources had been centralized and decentralized a few times in the previous couple years. Formal methodology had recognized value but we lacked agreement on a specific one—each team had their own set of best practices.

3. "Financial management" is, well, an embarrassing topic, as we were not responsible for managing project budgets. Of course, if a project ran long or required more resources than

---

17. The Agile software development methodology is a process based on iteration, rapid prototyping, and discovery of what is needed to build a solution through incrementally developing the product, feature by feature. I appreciate the Agile process because, in my experience, it helps teams 1) discover errors in thinking and assumptions faster, 2) place an equal value on each project workday, and 3) get the product to "good enough to release" faster than the traditional, waterfall approach to software development. For more information on the Agile methodology, go to: http://en.wikipedia.org/wiki/Agile_software_development

originally requested, we were held accountable, and by accountable I mean that we occasionally got yelled at. But we neither calculated nor tracked dollars.

Being a fan of David Letterman and his Top Ten lists, I felt that a Top Seven list would not sound as appealing, so I rounded out the list by adding my own three: PERT Estimating, Standard Process & Tools, and Active Risk Management.

PERT ESTIMATING

Standing for "Program Estimation and Review Technique," this is the process of asking for best case, worst case, and most likely case estimates when scheduling tasks. In doing so, you can get a much more realistic picture of how long a task will take, and the size of the spread between best and worst cases will indicate how much confidence there is in the estimates.

Try this at home the next time you ask your partner or spouse to go buy milk at the grocery store: First, ask for the single-point estimate by asking, "How long will it take you to buy milk and get back?" Invariably you will receive an answer of "Ten minutes." Then ask, "Just so I know, is that best case or worst case?"

What happens next is where the fun and beauty of PERT Estimating occurs.

With a head cocked to the side like a Labrador, your partner/spouse will respond with something akin to, "Well, that's best case. I'll probably pick up a few other things while I'm there." Your response might be, "Okay, so best case is ten minutes. Is the worst case something like thirty minutes?"—to which your partner/spouse will curtly say, "Sure." Be sure to smile in a loving way here, because you are on the verge of being annoying. Now say, "Okay, so the likely case is probably twenty to twenty-five minutes, is that fair?"—at which point your partner/spouse will probably pick up the keys, turn around, and leave for the store, since most people do not like the application of Project Management principles at home.

If performed as described above, you have just practiced PERT Estimating. You start with three point estimates—ten minutes for best case, twenty-three minutes for most likely case, and thirty minutes for worst case—and then plug these numbers into the weighted average formula below to get your Expected Time estimate:

[Best Case + (Most Likely Case x 4) + Worst Case] ÷ 6

Using the weighted average of the three estimates will give you the expected time, or twenty-two minutes. The theory behind PERT is that some of your tasks will come in at the best case estimate, some will come in at worst case, and some at most likely, and by calculating expected time you are baking contingency time into all tasks. For single tasks, PERT Estimating might not provide much value beyond setting a more realistic estimate. However, when you do this over the course of 100, 200, or 1,000 tasks, your project schedule becomes much more realistic. You will have greater confidence in your ability to hit the total estimated time. Plus, you'll have built in schedule contingency for when tasks go longer than originally estimated without putting your milestone dates at risk. In the case of buying milk, for example, twenty-two minutes will be more realistic than the original ten minutes given. Of course, it may take thirty minutes since your partner/spouse is a little miffed at you now and may decide to stop for coffee, but that is still within the worst case projection.

STANDARD PROCESS & TOOLS

At this point in my project, since I was an army of one, I felt that I should rely on the Project Management processes and tools I had found to be successful in the past and not attempt to reinvent the wheel for each project. When I found that one of these tools or processes was insufficient, however, I would proactively seek out an alternate, proven practice from a colleague.

ACTIVE RISK MANAGEMENT

For me, this meant engaging my team in identification and assessment of risks, not performing these tasks by myself, and frequently reviewing the list of current risks with my team instead of allowing the risk log to linger on a shared folder, never to be touched again.

With my customized top ten list, I identified ways to implement success factors on my project and then began evangelizing about the list to my Project Management colleagues. They also saw value in the list and began to look for ways to apply the ten success factors to their projects.

Through that first experience the Project Success Checklist was born, and since then I have altered my list several times as warranted by each project I've worked on. Over the years, I have found the checklist to be invaluable in the following ways:

Checklist Value Proposition #1:
Keeping my focus on what's important

Based on my own experiences, my colleagues' experiences, and the research data on project success rates, I am confident that the Project Success Checklist contains those truly significant contributing factors that make or break a project. By integrating the Project Success Checklist into my plan for every project I work on, and by monitoring its implementation throughout the project, I keep focus on those contributing factors that increase the likelihood of a project's success.

Checklist Value Proposition #2:
Project planning conversation starter

When I approach the planning phases of a project, I share the Project Success Checklist with my sponsor, key stakeholders, and teammates and engage them in dialogue about how to set the project up for success. When I have all the players involved participate in the conversation about success factors and identify the ways we can collectively increase our likelihood of success, I feel confident that we are focusing on the right things together.

Typically, I introduce the Project Success Checklist by saying, "Before we start planning out the work, can we talk about the things that make projects successful and things that make projects fail?"—and off we go talking about how to focus on success instead of preventing failure. It's an offensive approach, rather than defensive, and it feels good to focus on the positive. It's a great confidence-boosting and team-building activity.

Checklist Value Proposition #3:
Proactively identifies the significant sources of project risk

Each of the factors on the Project Success Checklist have their inverse—an issue that poses a risk to the project. Figuring out what those are is easy: take any factor and add "Lack of" in front of it, and you are on your way to identifying key risks to the project. For instance, "*Lack of* End User Involvement" shows that your first risk is creating something that doesn't meet the needs of the customer. "*Lack of* Executive Sponsorship" identifies your second risk as the possibility of having your budget cut or losing resources due to a lack of an effective champion at portfolio meetings.

Checklist Value Proposition #4:
Project Health Check Assessment

On occasion, colleagues and clients have asked me to assess the condition of a project or program and identify where potential gaps may exist.

The Project Success Checklist presents a great framework for assessing the health of a project or program: if the factors on the checklist are present, that indicates good health; if there is no evidence of their integration into the project that indicates poor health.

Checklist Value Proposition #5:
Lessons Learned Framework

Just as with the Project Health Check Assessment, the Project Success Checklist is a great diagnostic tool for a project's post-mortem review, where teams look back at project performance and identify how to improve their work in the future.

Checklist Value Proposition #6:
Project Management teaching tool

A couple years after the creation of my Project Success Checklist, I found myself in conversation with some of my Slalom Consulting colleagues about the value of identifying the key contributing factors to project success and sharing that list with our colleagues to increase positive outcomes. During the conversation, I brought out my Project Success Checklist and we began to modify the list based on our experience with consulting projects, identifying both ways to integrate the factors into a project and evidence of violating the factors on projects. We then identified the key activities we've used to embed these success factors into projects. We created the workshop materials and then invited the rest of the office to a brown bag session. We called the workshop *Why Projects Succeed* because it was about identifying and using those reasons "why projects succeed." Since then, I have gone on to deliver the workshop and presentation to numerous clients and industry groups, and I've taught it as an elective course within a Program Management Certification program at a local college. I've also written about the Project Success Checklist on the Slalom Consulting Blog. The feedback I have received from audiences and readers has been overwhelmingly positive, enough so that I believe the Project Success Checklist is a valuable concept that should continue to be shared.

When you create your own Project Success Checklist, I encourage you to share the list with your colleagues, not only to help them increase the likelihood of their project's success but also to improve your overall Project Management game. I will go into more detail about this later in the book.

LOVING THE PROJECT SUCCESS CHECKLIST: CONCLUSION

The Project Success Checklist's beginnings lie in the list I adapted from a conference keynote address, and its evolution has taken place over the years with the benefit of my experiences and the input I've received as a result of sharing it with colleagues. Since its inception, the Project Success Checklist has developed into a powerful tool for increasing the likelihood of project success for me and for many of my colleagues.

You many have noticed that I have been careful to state that the Project Success Checklist will *increase the likelihood* of success, not *ensure* project success. In the next chapter, I'll parse out that sentence to help make it clear that the presence of a Project Success Checklist does not ensure success any more than a checklist in the operating room guarantees a successful surgical outcome. I'll also stress the importance of defining what success means on a project by highlighting how one person's success might be another person's missed expectations.

KEY POINTS FOR CHAPTER 2:

- Tailoring and modifying the Project Success Checklist is how this all started for me; to increase your own likelihood of success, I recommend that you tailor and modify the list for yourself, early and often.

- A Project Success Checklist will serve many valuable purposes for you beyond keeping you focused on the key factors that contribute to success. These include building relationships with sponsors, stakeholders, and colleagues; identifying areas of significant project risk; assessing overall project health; providing a framework for identifying better ways of running things after a project is done; and sharing knowledge with other project managers to improve their capabilities.

- The presence of a Project Success Checklist does not guarantee success, it only increases the likelihood of success when applied appropriately to projects.

CHAPTER 3

Defining Success

Success is never final, failure is never fatal. It's courage that counts.

—John Wooden

LET'S MAKE A DEAL!

Given how hard we all work at *achieving* success, it is very surprising how infrequently we actually *define* what success means for ourselves and the things we do. And while the *Project Success Checklist* is primarily focused on the key ingredients for increasing the likelihood of project success, I would not be doing the subject justice if I didn't talk about the process for ensuring alignment on the very thing we are attempting to create. That said, in this chapter I'll first discuss defining success for projects, and then talk about what success means for you, the project manager, and how to measure your contribution to a successful project in a fair and compelling way.

DEFINING SUCCESS, PART 1: FOR THE PROJECT

A couple of years ago, I was on my way to give a Why Projects Succeed presentation (the previous workshop title for the *Project Success Checklist* content) at a client's site when a thought hit me like a two-by-four: the title "Why Projects Succeed" might set the wrong expectations in the minds of my audience—it might make them think that I was about to give them the keys to the Project Management kingdom, and that if they implemented these kernels of golden wisdom, each and every project they worked on would henceforth be a complete and flawless success. I literally stopped in my tracks and said two words. The first was "Oh," and I'll let you fill in the second word. I felt a pit grow in my stomach.

At that moment, the image of Prometheus popped in my head. For those rusty on their Greek mythology, Prometheus was a titan who created humans out of clay. Due to his affection for his creation, he stole fire and gave it to humans, which allowed for the creation of civilization, sliced bread, polio vaccines, air conditioning, and microbrew. As the saying goes, no good deed goes unpunished, and the theft of fire so enraged Zeus that he bound Prometheus to a rock along the ocean so the waves could pound against him eternally. As if that weren't enough, Zeus also had an eagle, his symbol, come to feast on Prometheus's liver, which would regenerate nightly so the scene could repeat itself daily. Yummy!

So, stopped in my tracks on Second Avenue in downtown Seattle, I realized that while I was about to attempt a good deed—just like Prometheus giving fire to humans—my efforts might be perceived as tempting the Project Management gods. When my colleagues became frustrated with my foolish attempts to deceive them into thinking I had the magic tools, would they bind me to a proverbial rock as well? As my anxiety levels continued to rise, I forced myself to reflect upon the key messages of Why Projects Succeed:

- As noted by Dr. Atul Gawande in *The Checklist Manifesto*, the use of checklists increases a person's likelihood of eliminating simple errors and achieving success.

- The creation of a Project Success Checklist is an easy and repeatable process based on tried and true factors that lead to success.

- The Project Success Checklist does not guarantee success, but instead focuses the Project Manager—and, in turn, the stakeholders—on performing the activities that, in their own experience, lead to project success.

Then it dawned on me: I wasn't about to give humans fire with my impending presentation—I was about to share with project managers the value of the Project Success Checklist, how to create the checklist, and how they could use the checklist with confidence. This thought allowed me to start walking towards the client's office again—and because I arrived with thirty minutes to spare, I was able to add a slide to my materials in which I made it clear that Why Projects Succeed was less a brain dump of "guaranteed" successful steps and more an invitation to project managers to actively increase the likelihood of their success. And since that day, I've told this story each time I've been lucky enough to give that presentation, because it sets—or resets—audience expectations and helps reinforce that the message of Why Projects Succeed is all about the audience member's own checklist and what they do with it. Success, after all, is not a passive activity.

I believe our true value as project managers is in the setting of, managing of, and delivery upon expectations. Unless we are actively engaged in setting project expectations, we run the risk of being caught unaware, possibly at an inopportune time, by expectations that have been placed upon us. At the beginning of every project, a project manager has a responsibility to set expectations for the project, and no expectation is more important than the definition of success. If the definition of success goes undefined, it can become very difficult to get all stakeholders to agree if and when the project is done, let alone whether it is a success. This lack of understanding about, and agreement upon, what success means will impact project team members' sense of direction. In my experience, a lack of defined success upfront means an increased likelihood of unmet expectations at the end.

In the next chapter I will go deeper into the value of and processes for setting, managing, and delivering on expectations, but my point here is that it is almost impossible to know what you are aiming for, what is expected of you, or when you are done with a project if you have not defined success upfront. It's that important.

How many project managers does it take to define a light bulb?

Speaking of checklists—a while ago, a colleague and I were creating a detailed project checklist around the specific steps that should be performed during a typical project engagement. Unlike a Project Success Checklist, this checklist was at the "brush your teeth, comb your hair," playbook level, and its purpose was to ensure that all the right steps were performed in the right order for each of the project phases. At a certain point, my colleague and I got stuck on a point on which we could not agree; I kept asking questions, trying to understand her point of view, and it finally dawned on me that we were in disagreement about the definition of "stakeholder."[18]

Now, the specifics of our misunderstanding (i.e., what our respective definitions of the word "stakeholder" were) are not important. What is important is what the experience taught me: when we make assumptions and don't define what the "common terms" we're using mean, we risk a misunderstanding. In the above example, the cost of this misunderstanding was twenty minutes of head-scratching debate and mutual frustration. But more importantly, the cost of misunder-

---

18. According to the Project Management Institute's *A Guide to the Project Management Body of Knowledge*, the definition of a stakeholder is, "Individuals or organizations that are actively involved in the project, or whose interests may be positively or negatively impacted as a result of project execution or project completion."

standing the definition of success might ultimately be the perception of project failure when the project delivers a different set of objectives than what the stakeholders expected.

One of the key points of this book, then, is the necessity of taking responsibility for defining what success means for a project *at the very beginning* of the effort and then leveraging the key success factors which increase the likelihood of delivering on that definition of success. Think of this in terms of a field goal in football: With goal posts firmly planted in the ground and the placeholder with the ball measured forty-five yards away, you can say that it is a forty-five yard field goal attempt and success would be a kick that puts the ball between the uprights forty five yards away. Clearly, a kick that travels only forty yards before hitting the ground would not be successful. Success versus failure is pretty cut and dried here. However, if the lines were to be removed from the field, or the goal posts were to be mounted on wheels and moved forward or backward, then it would be a lot more difficult to state whether a straight, forty-five-yard kick is going to be successful or not. The same goes for a project: project managers need to determine where the goal posts are *before* the ball is kicked, since it's a lot harder to control the strength and trajectory of the ball once it's in the air.

"Yes, I failed, but I failed at the highest levels."

A couple years ago I was thinking about how success is defined, but I wasn't in the office or facing a room full of clients and sponsors; instead, I was staring into the eyes of a different set of stakeholders: a team of nine-year-old soccer players. It was the end-of-season party, and as the coach, I was preparing my season wrap-up speech. I started to think about how I defined success for the team. The league emphasized having fun, so we coaches were told to tell our players and their parents that we didn't keep score or keep track of wins or losses. But of course the players and parents kept score anyway; I could turn to them at any point of a game and ask if anyone knew the score, and receive a correct answer. They also kept track of wins and losses: we finished that particular season with three wins, four losses, and one tie, or so I was told. Still, I never stressed winning; instead, I defined success by those things that we could control, and I repeated this definition at every practice and game to keep it fresh in my players' minds:

> **Me:** "What is the first rule of Space Monkey (our team name) Soccer?"
> **Players yelled response:** "Have fun."
> **Me:** "What is the second rule of Space Monkey soccer?"
> **Players:** "Be kind."
> **Me:** "What is the third rule of Space Monkey soccer?"
> **Players:** "Don't sit on the ball."
> **Me:** "What is the fourth rule of Space Monkey soccer?"
> **Players:** "Zip it when the coach is talking."

We frequently nailed the first three; the fourth rule was not our strong suit, but we did our best. But notice that these were all things we could control. Wins, losses, goals—these all depended on the quality of the team we faced and other non-controllable factors like weather, field conditions, and the amount of sugar the parents put into their kids before the game. But we could control our attitudes, effort, and intensity. We could control whether we forgave ourselves for mistakes. And if players were smiling on their way to getting their post-game snacks, then we had successfully achieved our goals. And we always did. We achieved our defined success criteria consistently throughout the season.

So, when I started to address the Space Monkeys at our end-of-season party, I started to tell them about Ryan Leaf, the former Washington State University football star and second overall pick in the 1998 NFL draft. NOTE: WSU Cougar fans, before skipping the chapter (or throwing the book), you might want to continue reading as the following might change some of your opinions about Mr. Leaf.

Ryan Leaf is best known for two things: 1) mismanaging the clock in the final seconds of the 1998 Rose Bowl as the quarterback of the Washington State Cougars football team, resulting in the team's loss; and 2) being one of the most anticipated quarterbacks to enter the NFL and subsequently failing to live up to the hype. (Keep in mind that I'm a UC Santa Barbara alum—go Gauchos!—so I have no dog in this particular fight).

With all that public failure, you might be wondering why I would tell my soccer team about Ryan Leaf when talking about success. Here's why: a few weeks before this wrap-up party, I'd seen an interview of Mr. Leaf, and he said something very interesting about success and failure. When asked about how he deals with failing so publicly, he responded by saying, "Yes, I failed . . . but I failed at the highest level possible."[19]

What he didn't say, but I will, is that in his football career, Ryan Leaf:

- Led his high school team to the state championship, something the vast majority of high school football players never achieve.

- Was a starting quarterback for a Division I college football team, a higher level of football success than millions of pee-wee and high school football players ever have achieved or will achieve.

- Broke the PAC-10 single season touchdown passing record, again putting him in rarified air.

- Led the WSU Cougars to the Rose Bowl.

19. Ryan Leaf's "but I failed at the highest level" comment comes from a *Seattle Times* interview and is a profound meditation on the glass is half empty/half full, or at least I found it to be. For the full chat transcript, go to: http://seattletimes.com/html/cougars/2016551631_livechat20.html

- Came in third in the Heisman Trophy voting for the season's best college football player.

Leaf failed on the field more than he succeeded? By whose count? If he were my son, I'd be extremely proud of his on-field accomplishments. His success rate at football is so much greater than 99.999% of his critics who squawk from the couch. So, is Ryan Leaf's football story one of success or failure? The answer depends on how you define success, doesn't it?

Here's how I wrapped it up for my Space Monkeys: "*Don't let others define success for you, always define what success means for yourself.*" *So my lesson for both* Space Monkeys and project managers is to actively participate in defining success and ensuring your objectives are based on factors within your control. If you allow others to define your success, you may be the next Ryan Leaf of the office or the playground. As I told my Monkeys, you cannot control everything, but you can always control your effort and your attitude.

In the context of a project, project managers usually do not have the latitude to define project goals by themselves, nor should they. Instead, success should be defined with full participation and agreement amongst sponsors and key stakeholders. Success should also be defined by those factors a project manager and their team can control. If your success is dependent on some outside force, you have agreed to allow someone else to define success for you, which means you are no longer the master of your own destiny. Don't let that happen.

MULTIPLE LEVELS OF SUCCESS

I hate the word failure. One reason is that we often narrowly define success as "attaining all objectives" for a given endeavor—and we are not always good at setting realistic expectations for those objectives.

The other reason I hate the word "failure" is because of the stigma that comes along with the word. The majority of our growth comes from making mistakes, and those mistakes often occur when we fail to achieve something. Failure, therefore—when not fatal, and if we are paying attention—can actually serve to make us stronger. As Robert H. Schuller once said, "Failure doesn't mean you are a failure, it just means you haven't succeeded yet."

There are some projects that are outright failures no matter how you evaluate them. But the majority of the projects I have been on have been somewhere in between "100% success," whatever that means, and 0% success. In other words, there is value in the outcome of the majority of projects—it just may not be the value that was expected or promised at the outset.

As far as defining success goes, most project teams do this in very black-and-white terms. The practice of measuring success by whether a project is on scope, on schedule, and on budget is a great example of binary measures of success; when judged by these standards, the project either was or was not successful, period. As you may recall, however, in Chapter 1 I provided two examples of projects that illustrated how success may be less black-and-white and more "different shades of grey." One project hit its scope, schedule, and budget commitments, but was a marketplace flop; the other project, meanwhile, met the expected ROI and company objectives, but had problems with scope, schedule, and budget. Neither project felt like a success to the team that worked on it, nor to some of its stakeholders, and both projects call into question the reasonableness of defining success in such narrow terms. That said, maybe there is a way to gauge projects based on different degrees or multiple levels of success.

Also in Chapter 1, I mentioned two studies that found sponsor and stakeholder satisfaction rates that were twenty points higher than the rate of projects achieving all their objectives. The 2012 PricewaterhouseCoopers survey[20] of IT projects found that 92% of projects met or exceeded their scope objectives but only 70% met their schedule and budget commitments. The Harvey Nash Outsourcing CIO Survey[21] found that 49% of CEOs were satisfied with their outsourcing projects but only 18% of those projects met their objectives. These are two examples how much a project's being deemed "successful" is based upon how you define success.

Recently I had a personal experience that really made me question my process for defining success in the things I do. Six months before running my ninth marathon, two of my running friends and I agreed to run the Vancouver Marathon together. Two of us were attempting to qualify for the Boston Marathon, meaning we had to complete the race in a fast time, and the other friend wanted to set a personal record by completing the marathon in under four hours. When they say "it's a marathon, not a sprint"—well, that's appropriate for marathon *training*, too, because you don't just go out and run twenty-six miles without risking serious damage to the body. So four months out from race day, we started running four to six days a week in the dark and wet Seattle winter, watching the foods we ate, and ensuring that we got enough rest. It takes a significant amount of work to get to race day—work that takes its toll not only on the runners but also on their families—but we persevered till the end.

On race day we were nervous, but also relatively confident that we could meet our goals. Well, at least my friends were confident; I had tweaked my calf muscle three weeks prior to race day and had not run since, instead spending hours on the stationary bike to keep my fitness level up. So I had some doubts at the starting line but was definitely willing to give it a go. After wishing my friends luck, I went to my place at the starting line and began running at the sound of the gun.

Miles one through four felt great. Then my calf muscle started to

---

20. PricewaterhouseCoopers, The Insights and Trends: Current Portfolio, Programme, and Project Management Practices, 2012: http://www.pwc.com/en_US/us/public-sector/assets/pwc-global-project-management-report-2012.pdf

21. Harvey Nash, *2007/2008 CIO Survey*, 2008: www.harveynash.com/usa

hurt—the pain was dull at first, but by miles five and six there were moments where I thought I might drop out. At mile seven I planted my foot on the edge of a painted line (yes, maybe only a 5mm differential between line and asphalt) and felt another sharp pain in my calf, but I recalled what a running friend once told me—"be in this mile," which means, "don't think about the miles passed or the miles ahead, just think about the one you're in"—and trudged on, keeping pace with my goal, a Boston Marathon–qualifying time. At mile eight, I thought I could do one more. At mile ten, my IT band started hurting, at which point I could no longer feel my calf hurting (pain is a great pain blocker). At mile eleven my quads started to also hurt, which made keeping my pace difficult. By mile thirteen, I had slowed down and accepted that today was not a Boston-qualifying day and just focused on getting through the next mile. At mile sixteen my hamstrings decided they wanted to be acknowledged too, and so the pain shifted focus to there. At mile twenty, I started to believe that the "be in this mile" philosophy might actually take me to the finish line—and at mile twenty-six, facing the last few hundred yards, I recalled my fears early in the race that I might have to ride a bus to the finish line, and I felt pretty good about what I had just achieved.

At the finish line, however, the reality of not qualifying for Boston started to sink in, and although I came in only thirty minutes slower than my goal time, I was disappointed. Luckily, before my pity party fully started, my running buddy who was also trying to qualify for Boston came across the finish line six minutes ahead of her goal time. There were big hugs and high fives over that—it's always inspiring to see someone set a goal, work their tail off to prepare for the big day, and then execute to plan. Then my other friend came over the finish line at four hours and five minutes—three minutes faster than her personal record, but short of her sub-four-hour goal. She was devastated.

Four months of training: early-morning runs, often in the rain; forgoing that second beer, substituting side salads for fries, and cursing the temptation of donuts; telling our spouses that date night needs to end at eight thirty "because I'm running twenty miles at 7 a.m. tomorrow." A lot goes into the marathon. So two of us were really disappointed when we didn't hit our respective goals. Our singular goals.

Upon reflection, I began to think that maybe the problem lies in that last line—the middle word there, "singular," do you see it? If we had set multiple or varying levels of goals when we had started training six months prior to the marathon, maybe our experiences at the finish line would have been different. For example, if my goals had been:

1. Complete four months of training

2. Have a great race weekend with my running friends

3. Complete a marathon

4. Qualify for Boston

Then would I have felt differently at the finish line? I tried on that redefinition of success on the drive home, and it felt awkward, like I was wearing my shoes on the wrong feet. I shared the concept with my running buddies and the one who, like me, had fallen short of her goal, said, "Oh, great, *now* you come up with that idea . . . *four months too late.*"

Retrofitting those goals post-race did not feel good, it's true; and I've been on projects where we've attempted to retrofit goals too, and they didn't feel good either. Still, I was convinced that if we had just managed to set multiple levels of goals early on, our finish line experience would have been much different. So I started thinking more and more about this concept, and I began to look for examples of where we already do this. After some thought, I came up with my first one: our educational system. Sure, we want our kids to get an A in every subject, but that's not realistic for most kids. So schools have a spectrum of grades, and if Johnny and Janey get mostly A's and B's, with the occasional C, we consider that successful, right?

How about looking at the airline industry for multiple levels of success? They have performance metrics for on-schedule departures and arrivals, customer satisfaction, and cost per seat per mile. However, when I'm flying, I make my determination of success based on my own set of metrics: Did I get there on time? Did I get the cheapest ticket possible? Did my luggage show up at my final destination? If I get two of the three, I'm likely to call the flight a success.

At the place where I get my car washed, they have three levels of service: Good; Better; Best. Each corresponds to a different service with a higher price. If it's been a long winter or I recently parked under a bird's nest, then I might go with the top end; usually, however, I stick with "Good." The point is, it's my choice: I define and then meet my expectations for a clean car each time I go there for a wash.

In customer service, complaint handlers have a technique where, instead of offering their own solutions to a disgruntled customer, they ask, "What will make this right for you?" This is an acknowledgment that the company's perception of what would resolve a problem might miss the customer's target altogether; it's also a clever tactic because the company's own suggested resolution might end up being more costly than what the customer asks for. And even if the customer asks for something that exceeds the company's threshold of a "reasonable" solution, at least the complaint handler now knows the perspective and posture of the customer's dissatisfaction.

As you can see, I found that gradations of success are used almost everywhere in life—a fact that makes it even more curious that we tend to measure success in such black-and-white terms in Project Management. We don't always proactively define success in terms we can control as project managers—and that, as both my kids would say, is messed up.

We don't have to look far to find examples within Project Management of acceptable thresholds of performance results. We often measure schedule or budget performance, for example, within a +/- 5% of baseline (i.e., we set upper and lower control levels for testing results). Perhaps we should be defining our entire project success using the same methodology.

So what would this look like? How about we take a page from my local carwash and create a Good, Better, Best set of goals for a project that looks something like this:

Success Criteria	Good	Better	Best
Commitment Management	Stakeholder expectations were set and managed most of the time	Stakeholder expectations were set and managed almost all of the time	Stakeholder expectations were set and managed in every instance
Benefits Realization	80-89% of ROI	90-110% of ROI	>110% of ROI
Sponsor Satisfaction	80-89% Satisfied	90-98% Satisfied	Completely Satisfied
Stakeholder & Team Satisfaction	80-89% Satisfied	90-98% Satisfied	Completely Satisfied
On Scope	+/- 10% of approved baselines	+/- 5% of approved baselines	+/- 1% of approved baselines
On Time & On Budget	+/- 20% of approved baselines	+/- 10% of approved baselines	+/- 5% of approved baselines

If you wanted to take this one step further, you could place weights on the success criteria and add scores to the potential results to come up with a numerical score for the project once it's completed. If you created goals for the aggregate score for the project in advance, this would allow for an objective measurement of the project's success.

When I present the idea of multiple levels of success, I occasionally hear that this approach won't work because team members will only shoot for the lowest acceptable amount of work—that goals need to be set artificially high in order to increase performance to an acceptable level. That may be the case in some companies, but I would argue that it points to a much larger leadership and cultural issue. My own experience has been that when I present multiple levels of goals, I am repeatedly amazed by employees' output. When provided with the right amount of support and autonomy, and when they are personally motivated by a project's objectives, team members deliver at the highest level possible, often exceeding expectations. This fear of the lowest common denominator for team performance happens in *Dilbert* for sure, but it's the rare employee that I've witnessed "phoning it in." Maybe I've been lucky, but I don't think so.

Now, I don't want to be misunderstood: I'm not saying we should give trophies to kids who only "participated" in their sport. I don't believe that sugarcoating results is good for adults or children. What I am saying is that success is nuanced. Sure, your team may or may not have won the league championship, but if the team excelled beyond expectations, you wouldn't call it a failed season. Even though I did not qualify to run the Boston Marathon, I did complete a marathon in which I thought about dropping out at mile four, and that didn't feel like failure. (Okay, yes, they did give out medals to everyone who completed the marathon, but it *is* 26.2 miles). You might not have delivered your project on schedule or on budget, but if the end result exceeded all ROI projections, would you call that a failure? By defining success on multiple levels, you can accurately assess the many complexities and layers of a project's success.

DEFINING SUCCESS, PART 2: FOR THE PROJECT MANAGER

Speaking of you—not only should you be actively engaged in defining expectations of success for your project, but also in understanding and shaping stakeholders' expectations of you as the project manager. Let's talk about how to proactively define your own success.

Successful Commitment Management

"You get the behaviors you measure and reward."

—Jack Welch

Clients and colleagues often ask me, "What is the most effective way to measure project managers?" Usually I respond with a quote borrowed from Chevy Chase's character in *Caddyshack*: "By height." But all joking aside, project managers are often measured by whether their projects are on schedule and on budget. And this approach is partially correct. After all, the project manager can be held responsible for the analysis and estimating process, the sequencing of tasks, resource planning, and all the other tasks that go into building a baseline schedule and budget. However, there are quite a few factors in those processes that a project manager can't control, and it's important to take those factors into account when assessing their overall performance.

A project manager cannot reasonably guarantee the quality of estimates, as those are usually provided by other resources who presumably have more expertise on the particular subject matter at hand. Similarly, a project manager cannot reasonably guarantee the correct sequencing of tasks, which is also usually prescribed by the subject matter experts as well. And the same argument holds for the identification of risk. This is why I personally never want my performance as a project manager to be measured solely based on whether a project is "on scope, on schedule, and on budget" because I don't actually control all the factors that go into that definition of success; I am reliant on the understanding and experience of my team. Yes, I can behave as if I'm responsible and accountable, and I may be treated as such—but do I really have control over all those factors? I say no.

So, what *do* you control as project manager? For me, the answer boils down to this: I control the commitment management process of setting, managing, and delivering on expectations. As project manager, throughout the life of any project, it's my job to engage stakeholders in the commitment management process to manage expectations on scope, time, and costs.

Commitment Management, Step 1: Setting Expectations

As we discussed, you can't control where you're going if you don't know where you're starting from. Of the three steps in commitment management, setting expectations is the most important. As a project manager, I have often found that key stakeholders in a given project have already formed expectations about project scope, time, and cost before I even talk to them. Knowing this, I strive to proactively identify those preset expectations and determine which of them need to be reset. I do this because I can't manage or deliver on any expectation of which I am unaware—unless I'm extremely lucky, that is.

One way I go about identifying these preset expectations is by creating a matrix of stakeholders and asking them what they expect of me and their fellow stakeholders. Once this is done, I review the Expectation Matrix with all key stakeholders, especially those who have not aligned on expectations, to ensure that all expectations are understood and agreed upon (I'll share more about this process later in a chapter on key stakeholder engagement).

One of the expectations I'm always careful to ask stakeholders about is their Acceptance Criteria, or what they want to see delivered once the project is done. If one stakeholder expects that you are developing X, another stakeholder expects that you are creating Y, and you think you are supposed to deliver Z, two of the three people involved will clearly be disappointed. Moreover, if Acceptance Criteria are not established at the beginning of the commitment management process, it makes it nearly impossible for all stakeholders to agree later whether the project has successfully met its objectives.

The accurate setting of expectations will both help you align your project tactics with strategy and give meaning and direction to those tactics. But expectations are not limited to your sponsors and key stakeholders. Project team members have expectations too, and they are just as important as the stakeholders'. Typically your team members will expect to know who is responsible for which roles, what level of self-guidance their team will have, how to identify and address risks and issues—the list goes on. As the project manager, you should ask for, understand, and actively clarify team members' expectations to ensure all team members are in alignment; otherwise, you may be adding "cat herder" to your resume.

In order to be a successful project manager, I need to manage commitments within my team, including setting the expectation with my team members that I will do my best to manage the commitments we make to our sponsor and all key stakeholders. If I am unable to do this, it will impact my team members in various ways: lost weekends and evenings, extra work, negative perceptions of performance, harmed reputations, and potentially diminished bonuses. Additionally, if I intend to hold my team members accountable for their performance on the project, then I must set clear expectations with each member. I cannot hold anyone accountable if I have not appropriately, accurately, and clearly communicated my expectations to them. No expectations, no accountability—end of story.

Commitment Management, Step 2: Managing Expectations

Once expectations about what will be developed, and how and when that will be done, have been set with your sponsor, key stakeholders, and team members, it's time to move into managing expectations mode. And while setting expectations is the most important part of commitment management, *managing* those expectations is the most difficult part. All of those commitments made during the first phase are now put to the test, and your project will almost certainly be knocked sideways at some point, possibly at multiple points. It's like you're playing Tetris: you have to constantly identify, align, and realign the pieces to make everything fit together. Put another way, managing expectations is like being the little Dutch boy who tries to keep the dam from bursting.

After your baseline commitments are made, you will manage expectations by providing evidence of attainment of scope and measurements of schedule and budget, and by performing risk and issue management in order to keep the project within its acceptable performance thresholds. Those acceptable performance thresholds should have been identified with your sponsor and key stakeholders when you were gathering expectations. If you discover mid-project that expectations cannot be met within the existing plan or performance levels, you will need to work with the sponsor and key stakeholders to adjust those expectations. You will do this through measurement, communication, evidence, analysis, and negotiation on how to recover from the variance or to create new scope, time, and/or cost baselines.

Allow me to repeat this point, because it's important: setting expectations is the most important phase of commitment management, but managing expectations is the most difficult. Setting expectations is the science of Project Management, whereas managing expectations is where the art of Project Management is required. Sure, there is the constant measurement of performance, controlling scope and requirements, ongoing communications, the detection and triage of change— but all of those activities require judgment, expertise, and elasticity. To do this effectively, you must keep your team motivated and on track, identify and resolve new issues as they arise, and then repeat all of it again the next day. Like I said: it's an art.

Commitment Management, Step 3: Delivering on Expectations

The entire reason a project exists is because of the benefits produced by the end product or because of the solution the project creates; that's why delivering on expectations is the final step in managing the commitments made on a project. In order to attain and validate "project complete" status, you will need your sponsor and the identified stakeholders to sign off—to agree that the project has delivered on all expectations.

To justify a claim of "complete," in addition to demonstrating the product, I will typically gather and present performance evidence to demonstrate completeness—not just the end product itself. This evidence can come in the form of test results, product documentation, sign-offs from project team members, and approvals from other stakeholders. More than a "Ta-da!" and some pleasing hand gestures, performance evidence plus a working product makes for a compelling presentation. You want acceptance and sign-off to be as straightforward as possible. It's a big deal, because without it you do not really have a hook on which to hang your "success" hat, so you want to make it clear to all involved that you've met success on every level possible.

To build consensus that a project is complete, I recommend starting before the project tasks are complete and the end product is delivered.

Instead of waiting till the very end, I like to start involving the stake-holders who will later be asked to sign off on the project in the earlier stages—throughout the development and testing of the product. That way they can experience the state of the product as we go, and have the valuable opportunity to provide feedback if their expectations are not being met. This helps me in both the managing and delivering phases of the commitment management process and is better for the project overall; the earlier we receive any negative feedback, after all, the more time we have to remedy the problem.

My favorite evidence of a project's completeness is to print a screen-shot of the final product (e.g., home page of a web site, front cover of a manual, a "future state" process map) and ask all the team members and primary stakeholders to physically sign that artifact. Yes, it provides a "suitable for framing, makes a great gift" item—that's the point. Once signed and framed, hang it in a public place to illustrate consensus of completion, demonstrate sponsor, stakeholder, and team approval, and build a sense of connection and pride to that final deliverable that everyone involved can share.

Case in Point

I was once assigned to take over a twelve-month, $1.3M project six months into its development. Our objective was to deliver a mission critical set of enterprise performance data for this particular Fortune 100 company, which was directly aligned to financial and marketing goals and was one of the company's overall key performance indicators for the health of the business. Once delivered, it would provide near real-time visibility and decision-making abilities for senior leadership, replacing the existing, very labor-intensive process which provided a two-month-delayed view into the company performance.

In the end, we delivered the project on time and only 0.24% over budget (no, that's not a typo—we were 1/4 of a percentage point over budget. Pretty good, right?). The sponsor, key stakeholders, and the C-level executives deemed the project a huge success; you would probably do the same if the story ended there, right? Well, if all you measured was functionality, cost, and schedule indicators, then it was time to print the T-shirts and have a party. However, behind the curtain, things could not have been more opposite.

The original approved budget was 63% of the final cost—not because that was what the team estimated, but rather because that is what the team had been squeezed into agreeing to. After I joined the project, I had to request approval for a 25% increase in budget—well over a quarter-million dollars—to make up for the unrealistic estimates the business product owner had "forced" the previous project manager and team into agreeing to. Furthermore, prior to my coming on board, when the business product owner had demanded more detailed project performance metrics, the previous project manager had responded by attempting to generate those metrics—which resulted in his micromanaging the team. Due to over-commitments of scope compared to schedule, overtime was nearly 20% of the total hours for the entire project. Morale on the project team was extremely low due to the amount of overtime and their perception of having been micromanaged; in fact, several team members said that they would walk if they found themselves on a similar project in the future.

Okay, stop the T-shirt presses! These are all the hallmarks of a failed project. What happened?

Clearly, expectations were not properly set at the beginning of this project for what was achievable given scope and time, and the project manager either lacked the negotiation skills to make the business product owner agree to more realistic estimates or the knowledge to appropriately elicit the support of their sponsor. Worse, expectations on how project performance metrics would be gathered and presented were not set or managed well—and even after morale was identified as a major issue, the right stakeholders were not engaged to address and correct the root causes of dissatisfaction. Team members have the expectation—rightly so—that management, and specifically project managers, will take care of them, and in this case that expectation was not fulfilled.

IN THE EYE OF THE STAKEHOLDER

If you define a project's success solely by whether it is on schedule and on budget, you will see behaviors that focus on those metrics. As Jack Welch once said, "You get the behaviors you measure and reward." But you may also wind up with a sponsor and stakeholders who aren't shy about telling anyone who will listen that your "on-schedule, on-budget" project was a failure. And as we have often experienced, success is in the eye of the stakeholder. Success is a perception, and perceptions are based on expectations. In the end, then, it is in everyone's best interest for you to get in front of the commitment management process by engaging the sponsor and key stakeholders in defining success and aligning their expectations for a project.

MEASURING COMMITMENT MANAGEMENT

As I mentioned before, people frequently ask me how project managers should be measured. Once I answer that question, I typically receive the follow-up question, "Okay, so how do I measure a project manager's contribution to commitment management?" This is where I refrain from using my *Caddyshack* joke twice in the same conversation.

Measuring a project manager on how they set and manage expectations with stakeholders can be done many ways, including asking the following question of stakeholders: "On a scale of 1–5, where 1 is 'not clearly set' and 5 is 'clearly set,' how well did the project manager set your expectations with regards to schedule dates, risks to the those dates, and potential ways to bring in those dates?"

Do you see how that question speaks to the complexities that the binary nature of "on-schedule" measurement can't identify?

At the end of every engagement, Slalom Consulting asks each client a short set of questions in order to measure satisfaction with the consultant and their work. Regardless of whether the project was ultimately successful, if the consultant communicated well and set and managed the client's expectations appropriately, the survey should come back with positive marks about the consultant's ability to appropriately set and manage expectations. This drives the consultant to both ensure the client is satisfied with the end result and to set expectations early on and clearly manage them throughout the engagement. It's an effective framework, and I do not see any reason why Project Management Organizations could not do the same thing with their internal resources.

In order to identify what to measure, a Project Management Organization should do the following:

1. Identify what's important to project success

2. Identify project manager behaviors that lead to success

3. Align those behaviors to measurable goals

4. Measure and report

My opinion is that commitment management is the Holy Grail of Project Management, so it should come as no surprise that if I were creating a stakeholder satisfaction survey, that survey would include several questions that measured the commitment management process. I already gave one example, but here are a couple more:

Indicate your agreement with the following statements, (1 being Strongly Disagree, 5 being Strongly Agree):

- The project manager effectively understood and advocated for my interests and expectations about the project with the other stakeholders.

- The project manager consistently provided clear communications on the current status of the project, clearly explained any variances to baselines, and ensured awareness of recent and upcoming accomplishments.

- The project manager provided timely and clear communications when unexpected issues came up on the project, providing impact analysis and options, and once a decision was made, he/she relayed progress towards resolving the issue.

Let's see—including the earlier question about setting expectations, in just four questions we have given ourselves a means of measuring a project manager's performance in the areas of schedule management, stakeholder management, status reporting, and issue management. Those sound like great areas to start with when measuring a project manager's contribution to stakeholder satisfaction.

Exceptions & Curveballs

Once in a while, you might run into a difficult stakeholder. Hopefully you won't, but just in case, in a metrics-based evaluation process, you will need to devise a way to account for the occasional difficult stakeholder who might use a survey like the one we've been talking about to unfairly punish a project manager. If you are not being measured already, you should be ready for it; more and more tools are becoming available all the time that enable better, easier measurements. Conversely, you will also need to identify a way to handicap stakeholders whose feedback suffers from "grade inflation" (giving higher scores than are objectively deserved). One way to handle this is to leverage a concept from Olympic figure skating: they throw out the high and low scores and count the rest. Another way to handle this, and maybe the more reasonable way, is to provide some human interpretation of the scores.

However you decide to handle these exceptions, if you are responsible for evaluating and measuring the performance of project managers, you should be looking for trends in the results. If only one of ten stakeholders has a bad experience with the project manager, the trend is more instructive than the individual scores. If half of the surveys indicate a bad experience, however, then what we've got here is a teaching opportunity (apologies to Cool Hand Luke).

DEFINING SUCCESS: CONCLUSION

I hope this has shed some light on a different way to define and measure success for projects and project managers. And I hope that at this point it is crystal clear that you need to be a proactive participant in the definition of your project's—and your own—success. Allowing others to define success for you and your projects is tantamount to abdicating your role as a leader and will likely lead to disappointment for some or many. Once success is defined, your role is to ensure that all commitments are managed appropriately throughout the project. Commitment management is not the easiest thing to measure, but in my experience, it is an infinitely better way to measure a project manager's contribution to the project than the "on-schedule and on-budget" approach because it drives the right focus and rewards the right behaviors.

Lastly, commitment management is so crucial to achieving success that I believe it should be one of the primary factors used to gauge a project manager's performance. The other primary factor that should go into measuring a project manager should be their ability to problem-solve and take corrective action when a project goes sideways—but more on that in Chapter 12. For now, just know that defining your own success and measuring your ability to manage your commitments will increase your likelihood for success, on projects and in life.

KEY POINTS FOR CHAPTER 3:

- You can either be involved in defining success or have it defined for you. Personally, I'd rather know what target I'm aiming for and have the opportunity to course-correct if necessary.

- By actively participating in the defining of project success, you will ensure that success is realistic and clearly understood by all stakeholders.

- Multiple levels of success allow for the nuanced reality of project success, and make it possible for all project sponsors, stakeholders, and teams to celebrate every aspect of the hard work they've done.

- Project managers should be measured on their commitment management performance—in other words, their ability to appropriately set, manage, and deliver on expectations.

- The standard measurement of project and project management success (the "on-schedule and on-budget" model) is too narrow and is not a fair measurement of a project manager's actual contribution. Measuring what project managers can control and influence makes a lot more sense than measuring something the entire team and other external forces will influence and impact. Just because something is easy to measure doesn't mean it's the right thing to measure.

SECTION 2

My Project Success

Checklist

WELCOME TO MY PROJECT SUCCESS CHECKLIST:

My top-ten list of factors that I have found to increase the likelihood of project success.

In this section, I will describe what each factor is, why I believe it is a top contributing factor for increasing the likelihood of a project's success, and how they could be applied to a project—and I'll attempt to provide a humorous story to give you some background on each one, too.

Again, the intention of this book is to inspire you to create and use your own Project Success Checklist; fair warning, my Project Success Checklist is tailored to my particular circumstances and might not be as effective for your projects as it has been for mine. I encourage you to do the same thing as I did: start with a list, add and modify, and make it your own.

That said: let's roll.

CHAPTER 4

Checklist Item #1:

User Involvement

As the saying goes, the customer is always right. That's primarily true because the customer's willingness to buy a product will determine if the product is successful. And the same can be said for your projects: you can't achieve project success unless your targeted users adopt and use the product of your project. Seems simple, right?

Even if you achieve every other Project Management objective, a project cannot be deemed a success if its end product is not adopted by the target users or customers. To increase the likelihood of adoption, you should involve those target users at the beginning of the process; if you don't, you risk developing a product that fails to deliver something valuable to the targeted user, which means a small "R" in your project's ROI calculation.

For this conversation, I will be using the term "users" to represent the target audience for the end product of your project. In your organization, you may call them stakeholders, or customers, but the idea is the same: they're the ones who will (hopefully) use the solution your team is developing. Now let's discuss some ideas for how to increase your project's likelihood of success by getting users involved, and conversely also identify a couple ways of how *not* to involve your target user base.

INVOLVEMENT

Users are great at articulating the issues and problems with current tools and processes, and at identifying the value of having the problems solved. The stated needs of users can be used to prioritize which features of a product get developed first. However, before you jump into engaging your users, there are some limitations to consider. Users are usually not great at identifying the most feasible or reasonable solutions, because they might identify solutions that address their specific symptoms and not general root causes of problems.

Let me tell you two stories from my past that speak to proper and improper end user involvement, and then we'll talk about some specific steps you can take to put end user involvement to work on your project.

Inadequate Involvement

Many years ago I was assigned to a project that was already over a year old when I joined it. The objective of the project was to develop a significant upgrade to a popular online application with millions of users. The team had done well in soliciting feedback from users about new features; however, the team was also attempting to develop a new platform that could be repurposed for multiple other products within the company. When the platform was originally conceived, the team had a "build it and they will come" mentality, meaning that they had not solicited the feedback of potential internal company customers for the platform. The team had not set expectations with senior management about the platform, its benefits, or the amount of time necessary to build the features and the platform.

Senior management was very interested in the new features but was growing impatient with the lengthy development timeframe, so I was assigned to the project to determine how to get the next version launched by a specific date. Together with the team, I determined that the only possible way to hit the mandated launch date was to delay further development on the platform until after the initial release and to focus on finishing the key features that senior management wanted. Unfortunately, due to the time pressure we were under, we underestimated the amount of time we would need to fully test the stability of the new platform—and that resulted in a big and very public mistake.

I once heard a speaker say, "You know your project is in trouble when it's on the 11 o'clock news." Well, that hasn't happened to me, but this failed project does have its own page on Wikipedia. That's enough notoriety for me, thank you.

While we did hit the launch date and the application was "technically" feature-complete, the platform was only half-baked, which caused significant performance issues—which, in turn, led to many users uninstalling the new version and reinstalling the previous version. Meanwhile, the new version was panned by the industry critics, largely because it lacked a stable codebase that would allow users to fully experience the "coolness" and utility of the new features.

If the team had worked with internal users at the beginning of the project to determine whether there was demand for an extensible platform, the team would have either aligned senior management on the value of developing out the platform in a reasonable timeframe, or would have received clear direction from senior management early on to focus on the "cool" features and not spend any time or energy on building out a platform that was not needed. Instead, a lot of time and money was wasted, and the reputation of the product and the project team suffered greatly.

Effective Involvement

More recently, I worked on an internal reporting tool project where the project team had extensively interviewed users to understand current limitations of their reporting systems. Users said the current process, which required manually compiling and reconciling performance metrics every month, was painful and time-consuming.

With this feedback in mind, the project team started by focusing on addressing the biggest pain points for the users: we created tools that automatically performed the monthly compilation and generated a report on reconciliation numbers. Users reviewed prototypes and their feedback was incorporated before the tools were coded, preventing rework. Lastly, key opinion-makers within the user community were involved in the testing phase of the project, which gave them a behind-the-scenes view of the product. This preview acted not only as a measure to ensure correctness but as a way to give key influencers the opportunity to get excited about the product and begin to act as evangelists for it amongst their peers.

The outcome of the project was a huge success, and the user adoption rate exceeded expectations.

KEY STEPS TO BENEFITING FROM USER INVOLVEMENT

There are several ways to engage targeted users early and often that will have a positive impact on the project. These include:

1. *Articulating Project Objectives*—Users can help you articulate the issues and problems with current tools and processes, and the value of having the problems solved. This information should be collected via interviewing. These interviews can also capture Use Cases, which are documents that outline the key user steps in performing processes with the product. Use Cases can be used as the basis for product requirements, test cases, and acceptance testing.

2. *Prioritization of Product Features*—Users can help prioritize which issues to solve first. Prioritization is something product managers and project stakeholders frequently have difficulty doing well. In 2002, The Standish Group published a survey of thousands of software products and found that 64% of the features were "rarely" or "never" used.[22] Wow! Think about that: Two-thirds of the features that product managers demanded and project teams toiled over did not add value. In fact, they actually took value *away* from the project because of the additional time, complexity, and risk each requirement adds to a project. So please, folks: if we cannot prioritize the features, let's rely on user feedback to do it for us!

3. *Prototype Reviews*—Users can help inform the design phase of the project by reviewing prototypes of the finished product, enabling the incorporation of feedback prior to development and saving time, money, and morale.

4. *User Acceptance Testing*—Having a group of users perform specific, predetermined tests that prove the product works as designed prior to the product's release can identify errors early on, giving the team time to correct those issues and ultimately saving the product from poor adoption later on. Plus, as in the case of the successful end user involvement project I just described, it can create product evangelists who will "sell" your product for you.

LIMITATIONS OF END USER INVOLVEMENT

Henry Ford once said, "If I had simply asked people what they wanted, they would have asked me for faster horses!" What he was referring

---

22. *Feature Usage of Typical Software Packages*, The Standish Group, 2002

to—and what's important to keep in mind—is that there are some limitations you should be aware of when engaging users. These include:

1. ***Problems, Not Solutions***—While users are great at identifying problems and needs, they are rarely good at identifying the most feasible and sensible solutions. Problems are easy; solutions are not.

2. ***Problems, Not Symptoms***—Users can easily identify problems, but sometimes those problems are actually symptoms of larger, root cause issues. If your team doesn't follow the right steps to ensure you are addressing root causes, your end products may fall short of solving the right problem.

3. ***You Can't Solve All Your Users' Problems***—Upon release, some users will remark that while the product meets some of their needs, it doesn't solve all of their problems. That's okay, as long as the product does solve the promised key issues. The issue here might be failing to appropriately set target end user expectations; even if this is the case, however, if you've solved important issues with your product, your users will allow you the opportunity to solve their other problems going forward.

USER INVOLVEMENT: CONCLUSION

The Customer has the ability to hire and fire you, just like your boss, so why not go directly to the source in order to determine the right problems to fix? Every project has the goal of 1) delivering solutions for customer problems; and 2) deriving value for your sponsors. There is no better way of ensuring that these two goals are met than to ask your customers or users to tell you about their problems.

I am such a believer in engaging users in the development of solutions that I created a survey for the purpose of vetting the title of this book. Tip of the hat to Dick and Emily Axelrod who were the first I've seen do this, and the result was *Let's Stop Meeting Like This*, an aptly titled book for improving the quality and results of meetings. I was so impressed with the idea that I knew immediately that I would do the same thing for this book. When I launched the survey, call it hubris, I was sure that respondents would pick my favorite of the titles. And of course, proving once again that there is value in the wisdom of crowds, you'll notice the book is not named *Why Projects Succeed*. Although this had been the name of this body of work for the six years of gestation and early growth, it was nowhere near as popular a title as *Project Success Checklist* was with the project managers who responded. Sometimes it's good to take your own medicine.

KEY POINTS FOR CHAPTER 4:

- Customers and users are great sources for information about the problem your project is attempting to solve by creating a new solution or product. Leverage users to better understand how they are currently working, the processes they perform, and what they want the new solution to achieve.

- User involvement can continue throughout the lifecycle of a project, from initial problem scoping and prototype and design feedback to final product testing and adoption and acceptances of the new product by trainers, evangelists, and influencers.

- Beware of the limitation of user involvement; as Henry Ford said, if he'd merely listened to his potential customers, he would have raised faster horses—not built the first affordable automobile. Your users and customers may tell you what they want in the solution, but you should be careful about the extent to which you follow that advice.

CHAPTER 5

Checklist Item #2:

Executive Sponsorship

There are two things you should know about the Project Success Checklist. First, there is no single project success factor that will ensure success if properly implemented. Second, in my experience, some of these success factors are just plain required, and their absence will almost certainly lead to project failure. Executive sponsorship is one of these absolutely essential project success factors.

Without an Executive Sponsor who is . . .

- Directly tied to the success of the project

- Appropriately engaged and aware in the project

- Actively involved in eliminating barriers and resolving issues

. . . a project is likely to be toast the first time the budget cuts fall, a new, top-priority project is initiated and requires resources, or a significant escalation occurs that requires someone to stick their neck out and fight for the project.

The role of an executive sponsor is straightforward, and a successful project manager knows how to engage the sponsor to ensure those duties are fulfilled. More importantly, the successful project manager knows that if those duties are not being fulfilled, it's time to call a time-out and have a serious conversation with the sponsor about the viability of the project.

The executive sponsor serves a vital purpose on a project, and their role needs to be clearly understood by both you and them. Generally, this is what I expect from my sponsor:

- Pays for the project

- Sets direction and objectives

- Makes key decisions and resolves escalations

- Advocates for projects amongst peers, engages stakeholders with concerns, and defends project resources

- Provides air coverage so the project manager can lead the project appropriately

- Signs off on project upon its completion

At the beginning of each project, I always make sure that my sponsor and I set clear expectations of each other. I am also careful to document what we've discussed so I have it on hand for future reference.

Having an active and engaged executive sponsor on a project is a wonderful thing, but even an enthusiastic sponsor needs to be managed appropriately. Here are the steps a successful project manager will take to ensure that an executive sponsor fulfills their duties and advances the project towards a successful conclusion:

1. IDENTIFY & REVIEW EXPECTATIONS

As I mentioned in Chapter 3, when you meet with your executive sponsor to review expectations, you should not only identify expectations for the project and for your role, but also validate the sponsor's role. Just as you must manage the expectations of any stakeholder, you will want to identify your sponsor's interests and expectations regarding the project and make sure they align with the goals of the project—and you do this by having a dialogue with your sponsor.

In this conversation, you should also get clarification from your sponsor about how they expect status and issues will be communicated, as well as how your requests for involvement will be conveyed. Sometimes these two get mixed with disastrous consequences: the sponsor gets involved when the project manager was simply wanting to provide "awareness" on an issue, not to get the sponsor actively engaged in the issue; or the project manager wants help but is not direct enough in asking for it, and the sponsor fails to get involved. In both instances, the project manager ends up with a result they didn't plan for, and this reduces their control over the project. The solution here is to clearly state your intentions up front; either say, "I don't need you to do anything about this, I just need you to be aware," or "I really need your help with something. I'm going to tell you the issue, what I attempted to do to resolve it, and why I'm now coming to you for your specific help," depending on the desired result.

2. OBTAIN ACCEPTANCE ON GOALS AND METRICS

The executive sponsor should approve the objectives and measurement for project completion, normally outlined in the project charter. The project goals should directly align with the sponsor's own goals, and the acceptance criteria should be definitively measurable so it is very clear when the project has achieved those goals and can be declared complete.

In ensuring that the project goals are tied to the sponsor's goals, you'll know that if the project goals are in jeopardy at any point, you will be able to get your sponsor's attention.

3. ENSURE ACTIVE ENGAGEMENT & AWARENESS

As I've already said, the intent of having early conversations with your executive sponsor is to set expectations about how you will be following through on progress and how you will communicate with your sponsor when you need to convey information or request their involvement.

You will not always be able to control the reactions of a sponsor, but you may be able to influence the appropriate response by employing some simple phrases, such as "I don't need you to do anything with this" or "I need your assistance with something." The appropriate use of a prefacing comment can help you put your sponsor appropriately on the front or on the back of their chair.

In the cases when you do need your sponsor to get involved, it will of course be easier to do so if you have kept them in the loop about the project's status throughout the process; that way they have the context they need to actually be helpful. In asking for your sponsor's help, you would be wise to come with a plan or suggestion for how they can help resolve the issue. This follows the age-old saying, "Don't bring me problems, bring me solutions." Of course, your sponsor might not follow your suggestions, but by demonstrating your ability to think through the situation and provide recommendations, you are showing them that you can be more than just the messenger.

4. GATHER SIGN-OFF UPON COMPLETION

If your sponsor has been instrumental in identifying and approving the goals and critical success factors (i.e., the Project Success Checklist) for the project, has been aware of the project from initiation through implementation, and has been actively engaged in resolving issues on the project, then this last step should come very easy: once you provide evidence of having attained the acceptance criteria, your sponsor should be able to sign off on your project without hesitation upon its completion.

So why even include this in the list? Because it is extremely important. Sign-off means more than allowing the project to be closed and resources released. Sign-off says there is no more work to be done—that the project has met its objectives and delivered on its expected value, and that all stakeholders' requirements have been met. And it means that you, the project manager, have successfully fulfilled your obligations to your organization and met the sponsor's expectations. Now doesn't that sound like an important acknowledgement when it comes to declaring success?

EXECUTIVE SPONSORSHIP: CONCLUSION

If you are successful in getting your executive sponsor to participate in and accomplish the four steps above, then you—and they—are doing a great job. But there are other things you can ask the sponsor to do to make for an even better project. For instance, you can ask your sponsor to:

- Provide motivation to the team by dropping in on project meetings

- Be involved in celebrating projects wins, large and small

- Personally recognize the contributions of specific team members

- Publicly evangelize and praise the project team's work

There are many ways a sponsor can positively impact a project, but you may need to coach and encourage your sponsor at times in order to get them to perform these steps. Remember, it never hurts to ask—and you should always be looking for ways to leverage every resource on your project team's roster, including the name at the top.

KEY POINTS FOR CHAPTER 5:

- Engaged and active executive sponsors are paramount to project success.

- The successful project manager not only knows how essential their sponsor's involvement is, they are constantly courting and interacting with their sponsor to ensure their awareness and willingness to participate when necessary.

- At the beginning of the project you must establish your expectations for your executive sponsor's role and level of engagement required to ensure alignment within the team and across the organization.

CHAPTER 6

Checklist Item #3:

Clear Business Objectives

"Would you tell me, please, which way I ought to go from here?"
"That depends a good deal on where you want to get to," said the Cat.
"I don't much care where..." said Alice.
"Then it doesn't matter which way you go," said the Cat.
—Lewis Carroll, *Alice in Wonderland*

A successful journey, like a successful project, requires many things, but one thing is definitely required: the knowledge of your destination.

On any project, being able to articulate the business objectives, the main reasons why you are undertaking the endeavor, is key to success. Like Alice not knowing where she wants to go, a project without a clearly stated destination will likely go in many directions, none of them resulting in the desired effect. Without clearly articulated and well-understood objectives, you won't even know when the project is complete—how can you, when you don't know what "complete" means or how to measure it?

Clear business objectives are important not only for measuring performance and declaring project completion, but for serving as the touchstone for all project decisions along the way. Business objectives help you define the triple constraints of scope, time, and cost, and they give you guidance for decision-making throughout the life of the project. Ultimately, having clarity about these objectives will make your project's "journey" a whole lot smoother. Here are the areas where clear business objectives are especially helpful:

FOCUS & SOLUTION PRIORITIZATION

Clear business objectives help project teams focus on performing the work that best achieves their objectives. Many times that will be evident through prioritization of requirements and scope—but when faced with a decision about how to spend project dollars between two efforts, being able to identify which one aligns better with the stated business objectives for the project will make the decision a whole lot more straightforward.

PROBLEM-SOLVING & DECISION-MAKING

When assessing options for resolving a problem on the project, the solution that more effectively aligns with defined business objectives should provide a north star for the analysis and help determine the final decision.

MEASURING FOR COMPLETION

Business objectives provide a measurement of scope attainment that helps you determine when the project is complete. One way to make sure your business objectives are set up to enable this is to apply the golden mnemonic for all goals, SMART, which stands for: specific, measureable, achievable, realistic, and time-bound.

In establishing SMART goals for your business objectives, you ensure clarity of understanding for each objective, measurability for assessing progress and completion against the set target, and feasibility of the objective and target. If you have concerns about whether a business objective is realistic, so will your team and some of the stakeholders— and the time to raise your concerns is at the *beginning* of the project. This will help you: 1) Better understand the rationale behind the objective, which will allow you to articulate support for the objective with any concerned team member and stakeholder; and 2) Determine if additional or modified scope, additional measurements, or new risk management activities need to be enacted in order to monitor and manage the potentially unrealistic objective.

Clear business objectives are paramount to a project's success because they inform the path you start your journey on, they help you make decisions when you come to forks in the road, and they help you declare that you have reached your destination. Without them, you may be wandering in the forest for a long time.

CASE IN POINT: MY EXPERIENCE WITH MUDDY BUSINESS OBJECTIVES

On most projects, the process of identifying and articulating the business objectives is a pretty straightforward process—and it's one that the sponsor and key stakeholders fully understand and embrace. However, years ago I was on a project where the business objectives were unclear and the sponsor was unwilling to clarify them for the team, which was causing all of us great concern.

The project was hitting all schedule and cost expectations so far, and had all the best resources in the department; it was one of the sponsors' top priority projects. I was assigned midway through, and when I asked why I was replacing the existing project manager, I was told that my predecessor was "driving everyone crazy" because he kept asking for the business rationale and drivers for the project.

That seemed like an interesting reason, I thought, since knowing the business drivers is actually a good thing; they are often inputs to the business objectives. So I asked a key stakeholder why the old project manager kept asking for the project rationale and drivers—and learned that the project sponsor had had made it clear that she was not interested in sharing what the business rationale behind the project was. When asked, she simply stated bluntly, "Because I want it."

After finding this out, I began to worry that I was going to fall into that same trap as the previous project manager. Still, I needed to know what our objective was, so I asked the team members and the key stakeholders why they thought we were doing the project. Nobody had a clear response other than "because we were told to do it." When I asked them how they would know if we were successful, they sheepishly pointed to our schedule and the documented desired functionality—but it was clear that they did not understand how the product they were developing would actually drive value for the organization, or how its functionality or quality would be measured.

I continued my line of questioning, asking several questions based on my Project Success Checklist:

- Had users been identified and a representative group of users been involved in helping to define a problem statement or helping inform the requirements for the project?

- Had the sponsor been engaged in the review of technical or functional requirements to ensure alignment with vision for the product?

- Had prototypes been presented to the users or the sponsor to determine if we were on track with creating a valuable solution to the problem we were attempting to solve for with this project?

The typical response I received from each team member and stakeholder was a blank stare and a muttered "No." One stakeholder even offered, "You know, these are the types of questions that the last project manager asked. Are you trying to get fired from this project already?"

My next step was to approach my sponsor. I requested a thirty-minute meeting with her as an introduction and an opportunity to provide an update on the project and share "my perspectives on the health of the project." In response I received a ten-minute calendar invite for the following day. *Game on!* I thought.

After a quick introduction, I told the sponsor that the project was in good status as far as progress to plan and attainment of scope, but that I had some significant concerns—mainly, I said, "we don't know how to measure project success or completion." I continued by saying that because we didn't understand the business objectives for the project, we were concerned that we might not succeed in delivering a product that would deliver value for customers and the company. The executive sponsor's response demonstrated that she did not understand why business objectives were important to the team and project: "Delivering this product will be fine enough," she told me. "Let me worry about selling the value of it."

Stepping carefully around the opening of that rabbit hole, I reframed my argument as follows:

> *Perhaps you are right, everything will be okay, and I'm just being overly cautious. But to be honest, I don't like surprises at the eleventh hour, and I'm guessing you don't either. This is a smart and capable team, so I believe they can be successful, but what if some of our decisions and some of the things we do are not in line with what's needed? For instance:*

- *What if the project team makes a mistake and they priori-tize requirements based on what they incorrectly assume is more important?*

- *What if the project team makes wrong decisions about how to resolve some of the issues already faced on the project based on incorrectly assumed acceptance criteria?*

- *What if the project team has been building features based on an incorrectly assumed set of success metrics, and that results in a poorly performing product?*

In my experience, clearly understanding the rationale and objectives for the end product helps guide the project team in the right direction. Perhaps they will guess correctly in each case and what you will see on the launch date will meet all of your expectations. But just to be sure, to stack the deck in your favor, don't you think we should articulate the business objectives to the team and check to make sure the teams' presumptions have been correct all along so there are no surprises on launch day?

(In case you're wondering—yes, I do speak in bullet points).

As I suspected, the sponsor didn't like the potential for surprises upon completion of the project either. After a long, awkward silence—during which I made a list in my head of all the things I would need to do in order to find my next job—she finally said that she had strategic reasons for not communicating her objectives, but she agreed that without "a guiding hand on the rudder," the team had the potential to go off in the wrong direction, so she was willing to be more involved in the project: reviewing and providing directions on product decisions, and participating in reviewing feature demonstrations as the work was being built to ensure course correction.

By connecting the dots between business objectives and the final product for the sponsor, and making her aware of the team's potential for getting lost along the way, I was able to help her come up with a way to keep the project headed in the right direction without divulging information she wanted to keep quiet. And after the first couple reviews, we did discover places where what we were doing wasn't aligned with the sponsor's vision, which made her more willing to participate in the reviews going forward. We never did learn what the strategic, backroom politicking that prevented the sharing of objectives had to do with, but we did launch the product on the target date.

While not my ideal way to ensure that clear business objectives would be embedded throughout the project, even in this difficult situation, we did figure out a way to make this happen. Yes, it was less efficient, and yes, the team felt disconnected from the business—more like cogs in the machinery than creators—but we did deliver upon the desired goals and achieved sign-off from our sponsor upon completion.

CLEAR BUSINESS OBJECTIVES: CONCLUSION

Clear business objectives highlight the destination for any project and provide a north star that guides the many decisions that will be made along the way. In order to eliminate surprises and ensure directional correctness, be sure to work with sponsors and stakeholders to develop and articulate your business objectives early and often in a project. And when you can't get that articulation of objectives, remember that discovering alternative ways to proactively ensure alignment with the objectives—even when they're "top secret"—is the next best way to achieve success.

KEY POINTS FOR CHAPTER 6:

- Clear business objectives are crucial to project success because they set the direction for the team, should be the basis for most project decisions, and provide a clear and measureable criteria for declaring a project complete.

- Business objectives should follow the structure of SMART goals to ensure clear understanding and measurability.

- Without clear business objectives, you run the risk of delivering a product or solution that does not meet expectations or cannot be declared complete.

CHAPTER 7

Checklist Item #4:

Key Stakeholder Engagement

Key stakeholder engagement is high on my Project Success Checklist because every project I've worked on has either been greatly accelerated by the help of key stakeholders—or hindered by them. As my career has progressed and I've taken on bigger, more complex projects, I have found key stakeholder engagement to be even more influential for project success. Key stakeholder engagement would be higher on my list if the top three weren't so vital: I need my users to inform my solution, I need my sponsor to set direction and knock down barriers, and I need clear business objectives to know the direction and destination for the project. But coming in close at number four is the key stakeholder, who has the power to support, impact, or even derail the project.

The common definition of a "stakeholder" is someone who is positively or negatively impacted by the outcome of the project. For some projects, that definition may include every living human being on the planet. For our purposes here, I will refer to "key" stakeholders, meaning the people who are directly influencing and impacting the successful outcome of the project; e.g., managers that supply resources to the project team; owners of dependent projects; business owners who will use or rely on the project; suppliers of inputs and receivers of outputs of the project; and basically anyone else who can knock the project sideways. I also make a distinction between "stakeholder management" and "stakeholder engagement" because I have found it difficult to "manage" key stakeholders—i.e., get them to behave in a way that is beneficial for the project—instead, I've experienced better results by taking an "engagement" approach. Engagement means first attempting to understand stakeholders' expectations and needs for the project, and then, if any misalignment exists, facilitating the process of realignment through dialogue and collaboration. By calling this "stakeholder engagement," I'm also giving myself an explicit reminder that what I want here is partnership, rather than attempting to manage or tell them how to contribute to the project.

Since key stakeholder engagement is a pretty big bucket, I have organized this success factor into three main parts:

1. *Tools & Processes*—These are the tools and processes that I have found to be effective when managing the various demands and requirements of stakeholders.

2. *Challenges*—Because not all stakeholders have the same expectations or perceptions of how they should participate, some will participate in productive ways and some will not. I've put together some ideas for how to deal with typical challenges that stakeholders bring into play.

3. *Communication Best Practices*—These are some ways that I have been able to better serve the needs and demands of stakeholders through communication.

KEY STAKEHOLDER ENGAGEMENT, PART 1: TOOLS & PROCESS

Earlier, I wrote about the importance of performing commitment management—the process of setting, managing, and delivering on expectations—and stated that this is the most important value a project manager can deliver to a project. Since whether or not a project has been a success often comes down to a matter of perception, even when success has been well defined and measured, a stakeholder's final judgment about your project's outcome depends on how well you manage their expectations along the way. Sure, results are real, and your final product is tangible and measurable—but even so, the way a project manager identifies and manages stakeholders' expectations and interests significantly impact those stakeholders' perception of a project's success.

When we identify the interests and expectations of all key stakeholders early in a project's life, we set a foundation for being able to appropriately set, manage, and ultimately meet all reasonable expectations for the project. When we don't do this, we are playing Russian roulette with our ability to deliver a successful project. With this in mind, let's talk about the process for identifying stakeholder interests and expectations.

Ask Stakeholders to Share Their Interests & Expectations

In order to identify the interests and expectations of a project's stakeholders, you can do something quite simple: ask them. That's right, just ask. Surprisingly enough, I have found that most stakeholders will offer their interests and expectations for a project freely.

State Your Intent

The best technique I have found for establishing trust and open communications with stakeholders is to start by telling them *why* you need the information. As Stephen M. R. Covey writes in his book *Speed of Trust,*

one of the foundational blocks for building trust is statement of intent,[23] because when your actions and results align with that intent, others connect those dots and your trustworthiness and credibility increases.

For project managers, trust and credibility are truly the only commodities that matter. Building trust with stakeholders will make it easier for you to engage your stakeholders in meaningful ways throughout your project—primarily because the stakeholders will be focused on the issue at hand and not be distracted by perceived trust and credibility issues with you. If you have not established trustworthiness with your project stakeholders, you—and, by extension, the project—will suffer what Mr. Covey refers to as a "Trust Tax": most things will take longer and therefore the entire project will be less efficient and more costly. Trust Tax issues you may encounter include:

- Receiving a greater amount of scrutiny from stakeholders when providing project performance metrics.

- Reluctance from stakeholders to approve project decisions or recommendations without more analysis, evidence, and measurements for the solution.

- Stakeholder skepticism when presenting analysis on triaging scope change or announcing rationale for delays in deliverables.

So, when you make it clear why you are asking about stakeholders' interests in and expectations of the project, not only are the stakehold-

---

23. According to Stephen M. R. Covey, as stated in *Speed of Trust*, the four core elements of trust are intent (why you do something), integrity (doing what you say you will), capabilities (being able to do what you say you will), and results (the positive output of your actions). I highly recommend *Speed of Trust*; it's one of my favorite books. Big thanks to Kelli Hildebrand for introducing me to this extremely valuable book. Kelli is an amazing instructor and presentation coach, and one of the more remarkable people I know. For more information about Kelli, go to www.keynotemoment.com

ers more likely to provide that information, you are building your foundation of trustworthiness.

A quick note about trust, also from Covey's *Speed of Trust*: the quickest way to earn trust is by demonstrating competency, which Covey defines as a combination of capabilities and results, and the quickest way to lose trust is through a violation of character, which Covey defines as a combination of integrity and intent. So yes, stating intent with your stakeholders will help lay the groundwork for your trustworthiness—but if the intent you state is inaccurate or you demonstrate a violation of your integrity, you are actually damaging, perhaps irrevocably, your trustworthiness. You get many opportunities to build your trustworthiness every day, but it generally only takes one instance to throw it out the window.

So now that you have collected all of these stakeholder expectations, what do you do with this information, you ask? The next step is to document, identify discrepancies in alignment, and share with your stakeholder team in order to build awareness and resolve those misaligned expectations.

Develop an Expectation Matrix

Stakeholders will not only have expectations for the project, they will have expectations for the project manager and even other stakeholders. Because this is a lot to keep track of, when you ask stakeholders for their interests and expectations, I recommend using an Expectation Matrix to capture the various expectations your stakeholders have. I have provided an example below from an actual project that has been slightly altered for use here (names and places have been changed to protect the innocent, so to speak):

In this matrix, all identified primary stakeholder are listed both on the X axis and the Y axis. Start with the stakeholders listed on the

Expectation Matrix	Executive Sponsor	Business Lead
Executive Sponsor		Deliver solid feature requirements, understand the users and their needs really well, be responsive to team questions and issues
Business Lead	Provide consistent direction throughout life of project	
Technology Lead	Be consistent in direction of solution, drive timely decision-making	Be consistent in the priority of requirements and engages user audiences to validate priority
Operations Lead	Approve budget for technology environments in time to procure servers for project	Be aware of timelines for delivery of new services due to changes
Project Manager	Be active and engaged in the project, be curious about status, solve problems for us at our request	Be consistent in priority of requirements, be engaged in issue and risk management, allow team to earn trust

Technology Lead	Operations Lead	Project Manager
Design a workable solution that fits into tech environment, assign the right resources, deliver the solution on the date	Ensure the solution will be maintained and supported well for service life	Communicate extremely well, be able to identify when a change has occurred, don't have to know all the answers, but how to get them
Ensure team builds a solution that works, provide good estimates and hit them, fix bugs immediately	Be extremely responsive to outages—prevent them when possible	Track schedule and budget closely, must know when we are at risk of running out of money or missing date
	Be responsive to requests for establishment of development and test environments	Protect the team from unauthorized work, know when a change has occurred
Good collaboration during design of technical solution		Please engage us as early as possible so we can better serve the project
Assign right resources for the need, address resource issues promptly	Be engaged in the project early so can plan and meet timelines	

X axis, and move right and up the matrix to map the expectations for each stakeholder. Once all the expectations are collected, you can review the matrix for any misaligned or different expectations and have conversations with stakeholders to address those differences.

In the above example, you can tell that on the project there were some consistent themes (e.g., the Business Owner has not been consistent in the prioritization of requirements in previous projects, Operations Lead and the Project Manager see benefits in early engagement), and some other tell-tale signs of lessons learned from previous projects (e.g., scope control). The value in capturing all the expectations and then sharing them back to each of the key stakeholders is that now everyone knows what is important to each other and if there are special areas of focus to which each stakeholder wants attention. As the project manager, it's invaluable to know this at the beginning of the project instead of learning it after an expectation has gone unmet.

This matrix is also a great framework for identifying the communication needs of each stakeholder, which means it can become the basis of your Project Communication Plan. I do not recommend merging the two matrixes, but you can copy the Expectation Matrix template in your spreadsheet, then open another tab and paste the template there. Then you can repeat the process with stakeholders, this time asking about communication needs and expectations.

Discuss Accountability & Responsibility

When meeting with stakeholders and stating intent, you should also spend a few minutes discussing accountability. I recommend this because there's a common perception that the project manager should be held accountable for the ultimate success or failure of a project, and I believe that is a misconception. As I've mentioned before, that view of accountability is too simplistic for me, as all projects are made up of a system of contributions from multiple stakeholders and resources. There are a series of inputs, processes, and outputs, and a number of external variables and drivers, that can have serious impacts on a project and are beyond the control of the project manager. To prove this point, let's look at the converse: When projects are successful, would you agree that there are many factors, drivers, and resources in addition to the project manager that contribute to success? If your answer is "yes," as mine is, then I think we agree that a project manager cannot take full credit for success—or for failure. And if stakeholders expect the project manager to be 100% accountable for a project, then that expectation needs to be addressed.

It is incumbent upon the project manager, of course, to ensure that all stakeholder expectations, realistic or not, are identified. A project manager cannot accept, address, or clarify any expectations if he or she doesn't know about them. Furthermore, if the project manager intends to hold their team members accountable for their performance on the project, they must also set clear expectations with each member.

The tried-and-true method for identifying expectations on project deliverables is the RACI chart. The RACI chart is a matrix that lists team members or key stakeholders on one axis and lists major deliverables on the other axis. RACI stands for:

- **Responsible**—the person(s) who performs the task or deliverable;

- **Accountable**—the person who is accountable for the quality of the task or deliverable;

- **Consulted**—the person(s) who provides input into the task or deliverable; and,

- **Informed**—the person(s) who are informed about the task or deliverable status.

For each task or deliverable, an "R," "A," "C," or "I" is assigned to the corresponding stakeholder or team resource.

The RACI chart is a great tool for identifying and setting clear expectations for roles and responsibilities on project deliverables. Just as important as the tool itself, however, are the conversations you'll have with stakeholders and team members as you set expectations about who is responsible and accountable for each project task and deliverable.

Stakeholder Engagement Tools & Processes Summary

The declaration of project success is often impacted by the perceptions of stakeholders, and even if you can clearly articulate your business objectives and what "success" means for your project, you cannot have a successful project if you don't manage stakeholder interests and expectations effectively.

In order to do this, you will need to balance the art and science of Project Management. The two tools covered in this section, the Expectation Matrix and the RACI chart, are proven to help with the science part. Next, let's talk about how to incorporate the art of Project Management when stakeholder-related challenges arise.

KEY STAKEHOLDER ENGAGEMENT, PART 2: CHALLENGES

In my experience, the challenges project managers encounter have less to do with overall key stakeholder engagement and more to do with specific issues experienced or created by individual stakeholders. There are three types of challenging stakeholders:

1. *Unclear Stakeholders*—those who do not clearly articulate enough or who are not open and honest about their interests and expectations

2. **Unidentified Stakeholders**—those who were not identified early in the project

3. **Unreasonable Stakeholders**—those who do not embrace what some refer to as "reason" and "the laws of physics"

Unfortunately, if you do not proactively identify stakeholder expectations and ensure clear understanding between stakeholders and yourself at the start of your project, you will only identify these types of stakeholders at a point of failure, and then you will be scrambling in recovery mode. So let's talk about each of these three types of challenging stakeholders and how you can prevent them from disrupting or derailing your project.

Challenging Stakeholder #1:
The Unclear Stakeholder

Now, there's a big difference between a stakeholder who does not articulate their expectations well and a stakeholder who is purposely not being open and honest about their expectations, but the impact is the same: you end up being surprised by their unclear expectations late in the project when there is not a lot of time to course correct. And there are two kinds of unclear stakeholders: the *inarticulate stakeholder* and the *less-than-candid stakeholder*.

An inarticulate stakeholder is someone who does not communicate their interests in and expectations for the project clearly enough—a failure that will cause missed expectations when the project is delivered. To prevent this, I recommend using the Expectation Matrix, highlighted in the last section. During that process, you will "read back" what you are hearing from stakeholders about what their expectations are and let them know that those expectations will be communicated to all the other identified stakeholders. At this point, the inarticulate stakeholder should, if their expectations are stated inaccurately, identify the discrepancy between what they meant and what you captured.

If the stakeholder doesn't mention or doesn't catch the misunderstanding at this point, then yes, those incorrect expectations will be carried forward into the project, because they will have signed off on the wrong expectations. But when you take these precautions, if the inarticulate stakeholder later says there's an issue, you can—after first scratching your head—ask them to refer to the Expectation Matrix (which, remember, they approved) and ask for their help in identifying a reasonable corrective action to fix the problem. You can even enlist the inarticulate stakeholder to join you in conversations with other stakeholders to help re-establish expectations. This is not meant as a punitive step, but rather a way to help ensure clarity with other stakeholders. (Okay, maybe it's a little punitive, because this will require more time from them—however, if they act with accountability, they will recognize their contribution to the problem. Hopefully without you putting too fine a point on it).

Special note: We will discuss fostering joint accountability later, but for now let me say that even if you do proactively identify expectations, perform active listening by reading back to the stakeholder what they said, and get all stakeholders to sign off on the expectations you've laid out, that doesn't mean you will be *accountability free* if a problem shows up later in the project. Sure, you've done a lot to prevent the problem—but even so, pointing fingers is never time or energy well spent. As the project manager, you should be focused on delivering the solution and ensuring the organization's ROI is achieved, not trying to prove you're in the right. Being "right" and being perceived as an admired, successful project leader are not always the same thing.

The second type of unclear stakeholder—the less-than-candid stakeholder—is someone who actively withholds information from you. You might be asking yourself, *Why would a stakeholder be less than 100% open and candid about their expectations?* Well, there can be many reasons for this. Sometimes it's because they have issues based upon prior experiences (for example, maybe they had a less-than-stellar experience with a previous project manager). Sometimes there are organizational politics at play. If one group does not have open and honest communications with another group, the stakeholder may be mirroring that behavior. Regardless of the cause, if you have a less-than-candid stakeholder on your hands, you need to act in order to prevent or minimize the impact of the stakeholder's lack of transparency upon the project.

Here are a couple of things I do in order to deal with a less-than-candid stakeholder.

1. I always state my intent with stakeholders, even those who I suspect are not being candid with me.

2. I tell a story-- in front of the less-than-candid stakeholder, of course—of a time when a project was negatively and significantly impacted because of a failure to correctly identify stakeholder interests and expectations early in the project. (That might be exactly what happened between this specific stakeholder and a previous project manager—even more reason to prevent it from occurring again).

3. If I still feel like there's a roadblock, I will call the stakeholder on it using the techniques called out in VitalSmart's *Crucial Conversations*[24]:

---

24. Crucial Conversations is a great book for highlighting a framework and approach for conducting difficult conversations. The book is written by Kerry Patterson, Joseph Grenny, Ron McMillan, and Al Switzler, and is offered as a training course by VitalSmarts. They also offer a free weekly newsletter with stories and advice on how to apply the Crucial Conversation principles. For more information: www.vitalsmarts.com

- I first ask the stakeholder, "Can I speak candidly about our conversation?" This asking for permission is a sign of respect and helps to demonstrate a desire to move things forward.

- Then I state a fact: "When you just said, 'Everything will be fine, I have no concerns with this project,' I remembered that the last time you worked with this team things did not go well—in fact, I believe that project was cancelled. I would be surprised if you have no concerns this time, and I think you might be holding on to your concerns. Is that what is going on?" By using tentative language, stating your opinion, and basing this on data or a fact, you are giving the other person the ability to validate or negate your assertion in a positive way.

- Lastly, I identify our shared goals by saying something like, "I believe this project has a big upside for us both. If it's successful, you will get a new tool that will help reduce cycle times by 25%, which will give you extra capacity to do some cool things with your team. A successful project always looks good for me. So, what concerns do you have about our approach on the project?"

Approaching the less-than-candid stakeholder with some emotional intelligence can sometimes thaw the frost covering them, but don't spend too much time catering to their deficiencies. Show them the impact, set the expectation for open and honest communications, document provided expectations and responsibilities via the Expectation Matrix and RACI chart, then be sure to identify and assess all potential risks associated with the stakeholder's less-than-candid actions.

Challenging Stakeholder #2:
The Unidentified Stakeholder

Have you ever received a screaming voice mail or a response e-mail written in ALL CAPS after sending what you thought was a generally benign status report? Something where the sender demands to know why they were not aware of a situation—perhaps a presentation made to senior management or the project kickoff? If this has happened to you, as it's happened to me, you've just been visited by an *unidentified stakeholder.*

When this happens to me, I accept full responsibility for the oversight and make every attempt to ask for forgiveness, and then I schedule a meeting with the stakeholder to identify any missed expectations and/or necessary corrective actions. Then I open up Stephen M. R. Covey's *Speed of Trust* for a quick refresher on the steps to rebuild trust, and I go back to stating intent and delivering results, thereby demonstrating integrity and rebuilding credibility.

The process for identifying all relevant stakeholders should be a simple one. The usual suspects are:

- Sponsors

- Project team members' resource managers

- Dotted-line or matrixed managers

- Associated program and/or portfolio managers

- End customers or their representatives

As you complete the Expectation Matrix with stakeholders, including the ones you might have "missed," you should ask if there's anyone else who should be included as a primary stakeholder. Then, when you ask stakeholders to sign off on the matrix, you should state that their acceptance also indicates that, to the best their knowledge, all stakeholders have been identified. That way, if an unidentified stakeholder should pop up and come at you, you can pull out the matrix and—after apologizing, of course—have an up-front conversation with the unidentified stakeholder about why his or her colleagues were not aware of their role in the project. If done correctly, this will not be perceived as a CYA move.[25] Instead, it will be seen as enforcing joint accountability, because you are pointing out that you *and* the other stakeholders missed this. As long as you are not defensive and you state intent, your actions should be received as helpful.

Challenging Stakeholder #3: The Unreasonable Stakeholder

The *unreasonable stakeholder* is—well—*unreasonable*. Every time I encounter a difficult or unreasonable stakeholder, I think about George Bernard Shaw's quote: *"The reasonable man adapts himself to the world; the unreasonable one persists in trying to adapt the world to himself. Therefore all progress depends on the unreasonable man."* It reminds me that even unreasonable stakeholders do serve a valuable purpose.[26] While these types of stakeholders might make the workplace uncomfortable, I have to thank them and their kind for sliced bread, bottled beer, and my sixty-degree lob wedge with laser-milled grooves. Working with an unreasonable stakeholder often creates the opportunity to be a part of something great because of what our friend, Mr. Shaw, has identified as the root of all progress. Dealing with unreasonable stakeholders on a daily basis, though, can make it hard to remember that you may be changing the world.

In my experience, the most effective way of dealing with unreasonable stakeholders is to not fight fire with fire, but to:

---

25. CYA is an acronym that stands for "cover your ass," and is usually an act performed when one's status and security is potentially at risk.

26. A colleague once shared with me another technique for dealing with difficult stakeholders: reminding yourself that someone loves them, even if it is only their mother. I've since used that a few times and found that it does temper my initial reactions to their behavior.

- Be open to their "suggestions" (i.e., demands)

- Maintain awareness of the approved constraints of the project and the impacts of those demands (I mean, "suggestions")

- Present options to them with time, cost, quality, and risk consequences

- Let them decide from the given options

In other words, if you can remain objective and aware of all commitments when contemplating requests, you can allow the unreasonable stakeholder to participate in a decision based on the options that *you* provide, meaning the decision they make will not send your project over the guardrails. For instance, if the stakeholder is asking for a change to scope, the appropriate response could be the following: "I would love to make that happen. In order for the project to accept that change, we will need one of the following: 1) More funding for additional resources; 2) To remove an equivalent piece of scope; 3) To add time to our launch date; or 4) Delay fulfilling the request until the next release. We will need a decision from you on that as soon as possible since impacts of the decision may change as time goes on. Can you give us a decision by end of today?"

Before providing options like these, of course, you will need to be able to evaluate and understand project impacts. If you are not able to do this on the fly, do not agree to or reject any requests in the moment; wait until you've had time to adequately assess the situation before responding. And you should never say no to an unreasonable stakeholder (actually, you should never say no to anyone[27]). Instead, give them the information they need about the impacts their request will have upon the project and let them make the decision. If they still want to defy the laws of physics, then you will be glad you have already established your escalation path,

---

27. For the experienced project manager, consultant, and lawyer, the appropriate answer is always "It depends" followed by a series of options with trade-offs and consequences.

and you will need to rely on the relationship you have already cultivated with your sponsor in order to bring sanity and restraint to the project.

Success is in the eye of the stakeholder, and stakeholder challenges, or challenging stakeholders, can definitely impact project delivery if not managed correctly. When you proactively work to improve credibility and trustworthiness, however, the payoff is better relationships with stakeholders. With unclear stakeholders and unidentified stakeholders, although you can take proactive steps to attempt to prevent them from popping up on your project, those issues that do get through your defenses require sincere apologies and a quick ramp-up to foster the stakeholders' support. The unreasonable stakeholder, meanwhile, can be rendered reasonable when they are required to choose from the options that support your ability to keep scope, time, and cost in balance.

KEY STAKEHOLDER ENGAGEMENT, PART 3: COMMUNICATIONS

If we're going to talk about communication, I again have to quote George Bernard Shaw, who said, "The biggest failure in communication is the presumption that one has communicated effectively." Since project managers spend a lot of time communicating—and much of key stakeholder engagement is dependent upon you doing it well—you should heed Mr. Shaw's warning and ensure your communication game is ready for prime time. With that in mind, in this section I'll share some best practices I've found that can either help to prevent or remedy stakeholder communication challenges.

Do You Hear What I Hear?

I recently read that a project manager spends 90% of their time communicating, and I instantly wondered how that number was measured. Not that I'm disputing it, but it did raise some questions: Was someone following project managers around with a stopwatch? Was there some cool, "communication pedometer"-type device on sale at the latest PM conference? But in all seriousness, once I thought about it, I realized: What part of a project manager's job is not spent communicating in one form or another? Building a schedule? No, that's a communication tool. Documenting a risk? Again, that's a communication tool. Writing a Project Management book? Wait, that's too autobiographical.

So, perhaps pinning the number at 90% is actually an *under*statement. But either way, I'm sure we can all agree that communication is critical to the success of a project manager. And since we're throwing out unproven (or shall I say *not disproven*?) metrics, I'll go ahead and throw out another sweeping generalization: 99% of all problems on projects have their root in a communication error. Here are some examples:

- Adoption rate of an end product is low because customer needs were not documented correctly (poor communication)

- Project is taking longer than originally estimated because estimates were based on assumptions that were not validated with Subject Matter Experts (lack of communication)

- Resources are not available for the project because true people needs were not communicated appropriately (poor communication)

. . . and the list goes on. I'm willing to entertain the notion that 1% of problems are not based in communication. I don't know what those would be—but I'm guessing the list would include natural disasters, your hometown team winning the league championship (and the ensuing riot), and/or a key resource winning the lottery. The rest are probably based in communications.

So, if stakeholder communication is so vital to project success—from understanding what you are expected to get done to managing expectations midflight to identifying when delivery is complete—what are some of the best practices that we can employ, you ask? Well, let's go over the three things I do to help prevent or remedy stakeholder communication challenges.

Stakeholder Communications Tip #1: Engage in Active Listening

My Slalom Consulting colleague, Carl Manello, cautioned in a blog post titled "Say what?"[28] that messages are often misunderstood because there are so many ways to interpret what is being said. Active listening helps ensure that you are hearing what the speaker is intending to communicate. The smart aleck reader might now be saying, "What I think I hear you saying is that active listening will help ensure what is being said is what is being heard, is that correct?" Thanks for asking; yes, that is correct! Active listening is the practice of rephrasing and repeating back to the communicator what you heard as a check for comprehension. By rephrasing and repeating back what has been said, you can eliminate a lot of misunderstandings and assumptions based on what you thought you heard or what the sender thought they said.

Most of you will be familiar with active listening, but my question to you is: Are you employing active listening as often as you should?

Stakeholder Communication Tip #2: Don't Be Afraid of Looking Stupid

When something is said in a meeting that you don't understand, do you ask for clarification every time? If not, why not?

The common reason that an individual won't ask a clarifying question is out of fear of looking stupid, assuming that everyone in the room

---

28. Carl Manello writes *The Art of Project Management* blog series on the Slalom Consulting blog. To read Carl's work, go to: http://www.slalom.com/thinking/

knows what is being said. But even if you think everyone in the room is following along, don't be afraid to ask the clarifying question. I have two reasons why:

1. What's more stupid: not knowing, or acting like you know only to be proven wrong? By asking for clarification, you will be able to identify expectations and act responsibly.

2. Someone else in the room probably doesn't understand either and is too afraid to ask. By asking, you will be their hero, and they may learn how to ask in the future.

Here's a twist on a common saying: "There are no stupid questions, only stupid people who don't ask questions." And I don't mean for that to sound derogatory. I'm using "stupid" to connote a lack of knowledge. By not asking the question, the uninformed person will continue to have a lack of knowledge. So when you speak up and ask for clarification, instead of looking stupid, you might actually end up looking brave and smart for asking the question that half the room was too afraid to ask. Good on you!

Stakeholder Communication Tip #3: Listening for What's Not Being Said

For fun, I'm going to list some of the most memorable things stakeholders have said to me over the years here. Each one captures some amusing and poignant learning experience I had during my career where I had to have thick skin and focus on the issue instead of my ego. And remember, what's left unsaid is sometimes even more important than what is said:

- *"Who are you? Oh, I don't talk to project managers."*

- *"I'm having a hard time telling the difference if you are being glass half full or half stupid."*

- *"Do you have any questions so far? Oh, that's right, this is new to you, you are too stupid to have any questions yet."*

- *"This is like a syrup truck crashing into a waffle truck. It looks yummy, but it's really just sticky."*

- *"A foolish consistency is the hobgoblin of little minds." (Technically a Ralph Waldo Emerson quote).*

- *"You come off very confident; even when it's clear you don't know the subject, you sound very confident."*

Yep, all those are real comments I've received over the years; what wonderful gems. Was I offended or insulted by each one? Admittedly, yeah, some of them stung, but there were expectations and deeper issues that lay beneath the surface of each comment. If I had reacted to each of them for the sake of preserving my ego, I would have missed key pieces of information the stakeholders were trying to convey.

So, instead of taking offense, I took these comments as an opportunity to ask clarifying questions and determine what was truly going on. For example, I might say, *"Help me understand that comment a little better. What is your expectation for me regarding . . .?"* In some cases, the stakeholder had information or a perspective I was not aware of, or vice versa. By asking for more information, we were able to share and come to a common understanding that would have not been possible had I let my ego get in the way. By asking the clarifying questions, you will validate that the message the stakeholder intended will be correctly received.

When I've looked beyond the insult, to the deeper meaning behind it, I have been able to uncover misunderstandings and missing information and, in doing so, serve my stakeholders in new and different ways.

One more sweeping generalization with metrics: A project manager will not communicate successfully 100% of the time. That should be expected. However, there are ways to attempt to prevent communication errors—and when errors do occur, if you can put ego aside and dig deeper with stakeholders to uncover what happened and determine how to move forward, everyone involved will be much happier.

KEY STAKEHOLDER ENGAGEMENT: CONCLUSION

Some might think of key stakeholder engagement as a Shakespearean play, with the project manager as the protagonist who attempts to navigate through the king and queen's court—through the politicking and conniving, through the power plays, deftly avoiding the poisonous potion in the goblet or the venomous snake in the grass. On my worst days, this feels about right.

On my better days, however, I find my stakeholders to be project accelerators, and sometimes even my best allies. When this happens, I can usually look back and point to the tools and processes I used to establish and manage stakeholder expectations appropriately, collaborate with stakeholders on the challenges that arose, and keep stakeholders engaged and supportive of the project. When I incorporate the above practices, I have found that I experience more "better days" than not—and stringing better days together usually leads to more successful projects.

KEY POINTS FOR CHAPTER 7:

- The more complex and challenging a project is, the more important your key stakeholder engagement plan will need to be.

- Your key stakeholder engagement plan will need to take into account the tools and processes you'll need, the variety of stakeholders you will encounter, and how you will be able to best manage the expectations and communication requirements for all of your key stakeholders.

- There are many different types of personalities that you will encounter on projects. Most will be great and will contribute to the success of the project. There will be some, however, who are threatened by the project or are unsure of how the project will impact them. While you cannot jeopardize the management of the project by spending too much time with these individuals, you will need to proactively engage and potentially mitigate their impacts on the project—this is where that aware and engaged executive sponsor can really help. Additionally, you may need to be able to read between the lines with these stakeholders because sometimes they will say things that don't mean what one might seem to think they say. Being able to dig deeper into those comments in a non-threatening, non-emotional way will help you get to the root of their issues and will increase the likelihood of a better working relationship—and, by extension, your likelihood of success.

CHAPTER 8

Checklist Item #5:

Professional Project Leadership

"Fortune does favor the bold, and you'll never know what you're capable of if you don't try."
    —Sheryl Sandberg, COO of Facebook and Author of *Lean-In*

To me, professional project leadership means something much more valuable than just being a project manager. Parsing out the term, a "leader" is someone who inspires and motivates others into not only performing coordinated actions for a positive outcome, but also going the extra mile, completing their tasks in the right way, and taking care of each other to make sure others are succeeding so the team can succeed. "Professional" is used here not to mean "getting paid for it," but rather to signify a higher caliber of performance—one that ensures the sponsor and stakeholders will recognize the value the project manager contributes to the project.

As with key stakeholder engagement, professional project leadership is a big topic. The first section of this chapter will help to illustrate the differences I see between a project leader and project manager, and the second section will outline two approaches that good project managers should adopt in order to become great project leaders.

PROFESSIONAL PROJECT LEADERSHIP, PART 1: THE SEVEN PRINCIPLES

When most people think of a leader, they tend to think of iconic figures from government, business, and sports—but not Project Management, for some reason (he says with tongue planted firmly in cheek). The thing is, while most people do not interact on a daily basis with an elected official, a titan of industry, or a professional sports star, a lot of them do likely work with a project manager. I'm sure you've experienced the positive and negative impacts a project manager can have on the lives of individuals in the workplace. The question is, have any of those project managers been project *leaders*?

Not all projects require the capabilities and talents of a project leader, and not all project managers are project leaders. So how do I define the difference between the two? For me, the difference can be summarized in one sentence: A project manager *pushes* a team to deliver on scope, schedule, and budget; a project leader *inspires* a team to produce their best work possible and exceed expectations.

While both project managers and project leaders will spend portions of the day playing taskmaster and schedule monkey, the project manager resembles the cat herder[29]—someone who is focused on being "on schedule and on budget," who attempts to foster teamwork, and who, despite getting a bit scratched up along the way, will get the job done most of the time, albeit with varying degrees of success. The project leader, on the other hand, will intentionally create a better process and experience, deliver better project results, and raise the satisfaction levels of the project team and stakeholders. So the argument for strong

---

29. In case you have not seen the EDS "Cat Herder" video, here you go: http://tinyurl.com/bt92lg. You are welcome.

project leadership is a simple one to make for those projects that require that level of performance.

Most project managers *want* to perform like project leaders, of course; the problem is, they don't know the principles of professional project leadership, nor do they know how to transform into a project leader. Let's tackle both topics now.

The Seven Principles of Professional Project Leadership

Here are the principles that I have identified that make for a Professional Project Leader. You won't always succeed with each one—I personally have both achieved and struggled with each of the principles from time to time too—but if you want to become a great project leader, or if you want to help mentor project managers into becoming project leaders, I suggest you embrace the following principles:

1. Advocate a vision

2. Engage the experts

3. Set expectations

4. Build trust

5. Foster joint accountability

6. Give recognition

7. Embrace change

Let's now go through each of these principles, one by one:

1. ADVOCATE A VISION

In order to inspire others to follow them, a project leader must present a credible and personally compelling reason to do so. Before we drink the Kool-Aid, we need to be convinced to set course for somewhere better than where we are today. Providing clarity of goals that are persuasive to the individual and the team, then, is an essential function of leadership. As I said at the beginning of this chapter, there is a clear difference between a manager and a leader: managers tell you what to do because of their superior rank, while leaders inspire you to do something by providing a vision and case for change.

A number of years ago, a colleague told me that "when everyone else on the project is freaking out about something, that is the time to go big picture and help focus everyone on that perspective"—and I couldn't agree more. In doing this, the project leader helps in two ways: 1) Their vision frames and provides relative prioritization of the issues, and 2) It helps align the resolution of issues with the overall objectives of the project.

By the way, the converse is true as well: When no one is freaking out about the project, that's a time to be concerned as well. While the project manager is out enjoying coffee, the project leader will be concentrating on risk identification. When everything is going smoothly and no one else is paying attention, you, as the leader, have the bandwidth to be performing proactive risk management (we'll go into this more extensively in Chapter 10) and searching the horizon for that rogue wave. So do it!

2. ENGAGE THE EXPERTS

A key trait of a great project leader is the ability to delegate as much work as possible to capable resources; that way, you have the bandwidth to take on the tasks and challenges that you are most capable of handling, that are your direct responsibility, or that your sponsor and stakeholders expect you to handle. However, delegation is not the key reason why project leaders should "engage the experts"; rather, the project leader should do this because: 1) It is the best utilization of available resources; 2) It makes for better project outcomes; and 3) It accelerates followership and team morale.

Hopefully, your team members were assigned to your project because their skills and capabilities are well suited to the work at hand. More than likely, those resources possess more skills and capabilities in certain tasks than you do. If this is not the case, then they were likely assigned to the project with the intent to increase their skills and capabilities. With this in mind, it is in the organization's best interest for the project leader to allow these resources to perform the work and get the intended experience. (If it's the latter case, however—if the team member is there to learn the skills—you will also want to make sure the schedule and budget is designed to accommodate the inevitable mistakes that will be made along the way). Ultimately, applying this principle will utilize the resources on the team in the most effective way possible.

Engaging the experts also produces better results, not only in terms of garnering acceptance of the project's product or solution, but in terms of increasing that product or solution's quality. In his book *Terms of Engagement*, Dick Axelrod describes the paradox of "old Change Management" as a few leaders making a decision and then attempting to get buy-in from the masses, whereas "new Change Management" should be a few leaders setting the direction and then engaging the masses in determining how to make this objective into a new reality. Mr. Axelrod argues that engaging key resources in the design and implementation of a solution not only produces champions for the change, it creates a better solution. The first precept makes good intuitive sense: you are much more likely to follow a decision you have been a part of the process in making, whereas a decision made without your involvement is harder to accept and may elicit some resistance.

The second assertion is slightly more questionable, however. Are decisions really better when more people have been involved in their development? In my experience, the answer is yes. When end users are involved with project team members in testing and providing feedback on potential solutions, the results of their participation always make for a better final product. That said, I'd argue that even if the quality of the solution developed through engagement is incrementally less than the quality of the solution developed by a few people behind locked doors, the increase in acceptance and adoption of the solution made possible by the greater engagement will deliver far better results than the solution developed in isolation. Engagement has a multiplier effect that can outshine the empirical quality; I'd rather have 80% adoption of an 80% solution than 20% adoption of a 99% solution, and those with their eye on ROI would too.

Applying the principle "engage the experts" also accelerates followership and team morale because of its motivational qualities. In his book *Drive: The Surprising Truth About What Motivates Us*, Daniel Pink identifies the three things that motivate knowledge workers after their basic needs (i.e., money) have been taken care of: autonomy, mastery, and purpose. Whether you refer to this principle as engagement or delegation, it fits nicely into Mr. Pink's autonomy and mastery elements, because you are giving your team members the autonomy to perform the work and you are relying on their level of mastery to deliver upon expected results for the task. Hopefully, as a project leader abiding by the first of the seven principles of project leadership, you will be advocating a vision that aligns the project objectives with the organizational values and mission—and if so, you are following Dan Pink's recipe for motivating your team, which should increase the likelihood of developing followership amongst your project resources.

3. SET EXPECTATIONS

In order to make it possible for each individual to successfully contribute toward their team's goals, and in order to hold each individual account-able equitably, a leader needs to provide clear and explicit expectations for each individual. Providing clear expectations also means highlight-ing the limits of expectations to ensure each individual collaborates well with other team members and does not attempt to take on too much by themselves. Rarely does an individual have a role in a project where they are not dependent on the contribution of another person; in order to accommodate that sense of dependence and teamwork, therefore, ac-countability should have limitations. Furthermore, the project leader should make the individual aware of the resources available to support those expectations.

In *7 Habits of Highly Effective People*, Stephen Covey, tells the story of setting the expectation with his son that he will be in charge of keep-ing the lawn green one summer. The boy (yes, this is Stephen M. R. Covey who when he grows up writes *Speed of Trust*) agrees to the ex-pectation but ultimately shirks his responsibility. Once the lawn turns brown, the elder Covey informs his son that all he had to do was ask for his father's help. Okay, great life lesson—in fact both father and son now retell that story in their respective books—but the end result was that the lawn was still brown for that summer. I would offer that the son would have learned the lesson *and* the lawn would have re-mained green if Pops Covey had simply told his son about the resourc-es at his disposal (e.g., his dad and the hose) before the lawn turned brown. If the elder Covey had used an Expectation Matrix like the one I described in Chapter 4, for example, then maybe the younger Covey would have known that being asked for help and support was an ex-pectation his dad had.

At the center of most conflicts there is usually either a difference in expectations or in perceptions of what has occurred. Douglas Stone,

Bruce Patton, and Sheila Heen wrote a wonderful book titled *Difficult Conversations*, which, provides instruction on how to approach, structure, and conduct a tough conversation. Their point that most disagreements come from different perspectives was a fascinating one for me; reading that, I realized that when I'm in conflict with someone, it's *as if* we're fighting two different fights because we *actually are*. If you find yourself at odds with a sponsor or stakeholder, it's likely because you have two different expectations or experiences. The first step to fixing that is to ask about their expectations or what they experienced.

By ensuring that expectations have been appropriately set, a project leader can create a culture of accountability. This eliminates a lot of drama and many of the inefficiencies caused by individuals who act without accountability—e.g., finger-point and blamestorm—when things go wrong.

4. BUILD TRUST

Trust is essential to healthy teamwork and is a key ingredient in high-performing teams. It's also the lifeblood of positive, mutually beneficial relationships that produce the level of efficiency and productivity achieved by great teams. Like leadership, a lot of us strive to improve our capabilities to be more trustworthy—but like leadership, trust can be one of those hard-to-define-and-articulate subjects.

The first step in mastering the mechanics of trust is identifying these mechanics. Fortunately for us, Stephen M. R. Covey has already done this for us in his amazing book *Speed of Trust*.[30] This book is so valuable for project leaders, primarily because Covey succeeds in so clearly and concisely defining the fundamentals of trust, and in identifying the behaviors that make or break trusting relationships. Covey identifies the four core principles of trust as the following:

---

30. I recommend *Speed of Trust* more than any other book because trust is so important to everything we do as project leaders, as project managers, as colleagues, and consultants; we can all work to improve or become more consistent in our trustworthiness.

1. Intent: Why you do what you do—an element of character.

2. Integrity: Doing what you say you will do—an element of character.

3. Capabilities: Whether you're able to do what you say you will—an element of competence.

4. Results: Whether you deliver the results you promise—an element of competence.

Covey suggests that the fastest way to build trust is to demonstrate competence, and the quickest way to lose trust is to commit a violation of character. As anyone who leads teams should know, be it as a project manager, the president of a company, or the captain of a sports team, people will only follow your lead as long as they trust your character and your competence. Trust is required to inspire people to stretch and achieve greater things than they thought possible, and thus a project leader must be trustworthy in order to be successful.

In order to inspire acts of greatness, a leader needs to understand the interests of the individuals he/she wants to lead and then align their objectives with those individual interests. Hopefully you've had the experience of having a boss or a coach who you would "run through a wall for." If so, I guarantee it's because you felt like they had your best interests at heart. But before they could understand your interests, they first had to build trust in order to persuade you to reveal your interests. How does a leader do that?

Covey says it comes down to four things: Intent, Integrity, Capabilities, and Results. Actually, I think it comes down to only one of them—Intent—because either you possess and demonstrate the other three or you don't. What I mean is this: Integrity, Capabilities, and Results are all externally visible to your team. Only Intent is something they can't see. This is why I share my intent with clients, stakeholders, and team members as early in a project as I can. That act by itself will not build trust—but over time, as I'm able to demonstrate integrity, capabilities, and results, my stakeholders begin to connect the dots between my intent statement and my behavior and actions, and trust is accelerated from there.

5. FOSTER JOINT ACCOUNTABILITY

At a large, matrixed company where I once worked, whenever I heard the phrase "shared accountability," my mind translated it into "no accountability." In my experience up to that point, whenever something went wrong, despite all the finger-pointing and flame e-mails written in ALL CAPs, I never saw any individual truly held accountable. Fast-forward a couple of years, and while reading Roger Connors and Tom Smith's *The Oz Principle* I came across a new definition of "joint accountability" that still really resonates with me. Simply put, Mr. Connors and Mr. Smith say that in order to create a culture of joint accountability, a leader must demand that every team member ask two questions when a problem occurs:

1. What did I do to help contribute to the problem

2. What can we do to move toward desired results?

With that as the framework, anytime anyone is doing anything other than asking those two questions after something has gone wrong, they are not acting with personal accountability.

Fostering joint accountability means *informing others when they are not acting with accountability*. Instead of yelling at someone when they haven't done what they agreed to do (to which they will most likely respond by making excuses and going on the defensive), you just have to remind them that they are not acting with accountability. By helping the individual re-focus on those two important questions—*How did I contribute?* and *What can we do to move forward?*—you will cultivate a culture of joint accountability and ultimately help your team to be more proactive and constructive. Embracing the concept of joint accountability reflects a reality where, most of the time, tasks and deliverables for projects are dependent on inputs from multiple people.

On our projects, if following good practices, we'll create RACI charts to highlight who is accountable and who is responsible for performing the work, we'll assign ownership to tasks and issues, and we'll throw around the concept of *"single throat to choke"* as a sort of homage to a more draconian style of accountability. Although the focus is on trying to get to single accountability, rarely are tasks so independent that anyone truly "owns" something. Between inputs and outputs, hand-offs, poor communication, lack of thorough planning, and Garbage-In/Garbage-Out realities, we are too interdependent in project environments for any one individual to be fully, *independently* accountable. And enforcing accountability *after* something goes wrong is far more costly and inefficient than simply inspiring people to act with accountability in the first place.

As project leaders, we will frequently encounter problems, so as a standard practice we should demonstrate our own personal accountability by asking those two questions—how we have contributed to the problem, and how we can move forward—of ourselves publicly. To foster joint accountability we should remind others who forget those two questions to act with accountability. When individuals on a team hold each other jointly accountable in a positive way, behavioral changes occur that strengthen the team dynamic and increase productivity rather than tear the team down in a defensive game of blamestorming. [31]

---

31. Dictionary.com defines blamestorming as "a discussion or meeting for the purpose of assigning blame." These are useless meetings, no matter how fun they might be.

6. GIVE RECOGNITION

The first principle of professional project leadership, as you might re-member, is to advocate a vision. Earlier, I wrote that when a project leader articulates their vision, they must be able to tell a compelling sto-ry that connects the individual to the objective—and in order to create that compelling story, a leader must understand the interests of the in-dividuals. In *The Carrot Principle*, authors Adrian Gostick and Chester Elton suggest that leaders who are 1) able to connect individual interests and accomplishments with a project's objectives, and 2) able to provide immediate acknowledgement of the achievement will greatly accelerate the productivity and performance of their team. I have seen a few lead-ers in my day whose praise for individuals' contributions to the team's objectives and their goals not only resulted in better performances but also led to team members holding themselves to a higher standard of accountability than before. Those experiences made me a believer.

Let me give you two personal examples where recognition, depend-ing on whether it is connected to a person's interests, has either a nega-tive or positive effect:

- I can do the dishes at home extremely efficiently. No full sink takes me longer than ten minutes to clean and stack. But let's be clear: dishes are not one of my interests. In fact, I do not enjoy doing the dishes. While it's important to us as a family to have a clean dishes, whenever my wife thanks me for doing the dishes, it doesn't resonate or give me a level of satisfaction as much as when I am recognized for doing something well when I really love doing that thing.

- Something else I'm good at: I can take complex subjects and scenarios, break them down into digestible concepts and frameworks, present them back to audiences at different levels, and create new degrees of understanding. I love doing this. When my client or boss tells me I did a great job at a presentation, I'm floating for a week.

See the difference? In the first example, I have received recognition for doing something I don't like to do, so I'm not going to be any more motivated to do the dishes next time. In the second example, I've been praised for something I enjoy doing, and it makes me want to start working on the next class. Recognition is only an accelerator for the things I like to do.

As a project leader, then, if you want the best from the individuals on your team, you need to find out what excites them, catch them doing that and doing it well, and then recognize them for that contribution. It will fuel the fire for greater achievements and drive great performance on your project today.

7. EMBRACE CHANGE

Leaders are there to either reinforce a prior change or to drive a team to a new reality. In order to achieve either, a leader not only needs to *advocate the vision* for change but to know how to *execute the change* which will be more successful by using a proven framework and tools for producing change in individuals, teams, processes, and systems. But change is hard. And like anything in life, it comes down to attitude and approach. There are two types of change a leader must embrace: unplanned and desired change.

Unplanned change is why every project should have a plan on how to manage scope change. I've never met a project manager who didn't have at least one thing knock their project sideways at some point in the process, and from an approach standpoint, this is why project leaders ensure baselines and control thresholds are developed: to identify when changes have occurred, and to have a framework for knowing what to do with those changes. Therefore, a project leader should expect change and be flexible in tactics, but unyielding for the objectives.

Desired change is the other side of the coin. Isn't that the name of the game for leaders, after all—to lead people to a new reality? Project leaders should embrace the principles of organizational change management and know how to integrate those tactics into their project plan. Ultimately, this will allow you to lead your team through meaningful change and achieve project objectives. I'll say more about project leaders and organizational change management in Chapter 14.

PROFESSIONAL PROJECT LEADERSHIP, PART 1: SUMMARY

To build upon a line from Shakespeare: project leaders who have "greatness thrust upon them" have not hit the leadership lottery. They've done their prep work. They've set clear expectations, built trust, and fostered accountability. They've embraced rather than run from change. And they have, first and foremost, provided a clear and compelling vision that drives all the leadership principles presented here. Individuals who find themselves in a project manager position have two choices available to them: they can either manage in Sisyphean fashion, pushing that stone uphill in attempt to hit their schedule and budget goals, or they can inspire their team to produce something of value that they all can be proud of. Managers push people, leaders pull. As individuals, we naturally resist when pushed—but we flow toward those things that pull us, those things that offer a reward or give us more autonomy and mastery.

With that *pull* mentality in mind, I've outlined two approaches that good project managers can adopt in order to become great project leaders. The intent is to provide the approach for making these principles actionable and helping our good project managers on their way to achieving inspired followership.

PROFESSIONAL PROJECT LEADERSHIP, PART 2: PROJECT LEADER APPROACHES

"Leaders aren't born, they are made. And they are made just like anything else, through hard work. And that's the price we'll have to pay to achieve that goal, or any goal."

—Vince Lombardi

I find the building blocks of leadership to be quite simple to articulate. The real challenge is incorporating these principles into your professional practice as a project manager. Just like greatness, it can be easy to spot, but hard to emulate.

I define a successful project manager as someone who:

- Succinctly identifies stakeholder interests and expectations and appropriately drives the commitment management process (setting, managing, and delivering of expectations)

- Pushes the team to deliver on scope, schedule, and budget expectations

- Effectively marshals the team efforts to triage and course correct when the project is knocked sideways

- Daily fosters team work and accountability

- Positively influences and guides a project to a successful and satisfactory conclusion

By this definition, a successful project manager has some innate leadership traits, or is extremely lucky. Assuming it's the former, in order to become a great project leader—someone who inspires others to achieve great things and doesn't just push them to the finish line—you need to ignite your booster rockets. The fuel you need to do this has three parts: awareness, intention, and focus. Since I've covered the principles above, color yourself *aware*. Now, let's discuss the intention and focus a project manager needs to have in order to become aproject leader.

Be Intentional

"*The more I practice, the luckier I become.*"

—Arnold Palmer

Excellence is achieved through the following combination: a good plan, great preparation, solid execution, and a few things going right at crucial moments. While project leaders cannot create lucky breaks, they can be intentional in how they plan and prepare so that when a lucky break does happen, they can take full advantage of it. Does this mean that project leaders create leadership moments? Yes, yes it does. Throughout the course of a project, there are always a number of moments, both large and small, that project managers can use to build upon the leadership principles.

To become a leader, a project manager must be intentional about creating leadership moments. These are mostly going to be small moments early in the project when typical pressures focus on "starting work" and "getting busy." Planning and preparation are rarely seen as part of the "doing" of work—but the truth is, every great achievement starts with a good plan. Here are some examples of small moments a project leader will intentionally perform as part of their preparations for success:

- *Identifying team member and stakeholder interests*—Aligning interests with objectives enables the leader to articulate a *vision*, provide meaningful *recognition*.

- ***Stating intent early in projects***—When aligned with demonstrated integrity, capabilities, and results, stating intent accelerates *trust.*

- ***Creating awareness of expectations***—Working with key stakeholders and team members to explicitly identify and clearly articulate *expectations* is the central building block for a culture of *accountability.*

- ***Softening the target***—Incorporating organizational change management principles ensures adoption of the planned *change* resulting from the product of the project.

Another way project leaders can be intentional is in the choosing of the tasks and projects that they focus their energies on. And this is not just about *"picking your battles"* (although that is part of it). This concept is about leaders being intentional about where they spend their energies and focus their strengths, and "partnering" with others on any tasks or projects that are not in their wheelhouse.

A simple example of this is meeting notes. No one will disagree that documenting issues, action items, and decisions should be a requirement of all meetings; however, not everyone likes taking notes or is good at it, and nowhere is it written that the project manager has to take on this responsibility. This task can be delegated to another individual, or it can be shared amongst the regular meeting attendees.

For a more significant example of delegating tasks, I draw upon an experience that a colleague of mine had. She was drowning in a sea of unmet expectations and an ever-increasing action item list, and she knew something had to change. She loved the role she had picked for herself, but after a couple of months, she thought she might not be up for the responsibilities of the position, because she wasn't getting everything done. In fact, she was ready to quit, lick her wounds, and start again a couple rungs lower in the organization. Luckily, she had a manager who recognized the symptoms and could prescribe the treatment. The manager informed my colleague that she had "*Big Eye*-itis," a self-inflicted injury leaders incur when they sign up for too much work in multiple areas, which is a recipe for conflicting priorities and not enough hours in the day. The prescribed treatment: building and completing a matrix (we are consultants, right?) with the following columns:

Criteria	Description
Tasks/ Responsibilities	Identify tasks or responsibilities you had for the last month. You can choose how granular you want to be here.
Planned % of Time	Indicate how much time you plan for this task or responsibility for the last month.
Actual % of Time	Indicate how much time you spent on this task or responsibility for the last month.
Personal Goal Rank	Indicate how important the task is to you and your personal/career goals. If you don't have personal/career goals, you need to determine what they are; only then can you be intentional about achieving them.

▶

Criteria	Description
Business Goal Rank	Indicate how important the task is to your business goals or your company's goals.
I Love/Loathe It	Indicate if you truly enjoy performing the task or if you detest the task.
Action Plan	Based on your analysis, indicate what steps you can take to address any issues.

The most important column in this matrix is the "Love/Loathe" designation. This is a concept that Marcus Buckingham has championed in his body of work on "strengths"—*Now, Discover Your Strengths, Go Put Your Strengths to Work,* and several others. He defines a strength as a task that invigorates us and gives us energy—something that we jump to do. "Strengths" are not only what we are good at, then, but what we are passionate about and have talent for. There are activities we might be recognized as being good at, or even excelling at, but if we cringe at them when we see them on our to-do list, Mr. Buckingham says, they are "weaknesses"; like Kryptonite does to Superman, they exhaust our energies and drain our superpowers.

Marcus Buckingham is quick to point out that you will never remove all of the activities that "drain you" from your list; however, as a leader, your goal should be to move these off your list as quickly as possible. This can be done in three ways: eliminating, delegating, or partnering. If the task does not generate value and is not required, eliminate it. If the task is important (high on your list of business goals, does generate value, or is required), delegate it or partner with someone for whom the task utilizes their "strengths."

Of course, the responses in the other columns in this matrix are informative, too:

● ***Personal vs. Business Goals***—If there is a disconnect between personal and business goals, the individual should have a discussion with their manager to reset expectations or possibly find a role better suited to their abilities.

● ***Planned vs. Actual***—Disconnects identified here may help the individual adjust their focus on these activities up or down as appropriate.

To be effective, all leaders need to be intentional about how they balance their priorities and ensure that their best effort is put in the areas of highest impact. After completing this matrix, my colleague quickly identified what she needed to do and which activities she needed to perform more frequently in order to achieve a higher sense of accomplishment and achievement, and thus be a more effective leader. She also identified those activities that she needed to remove from her plate. Since executing the actions she identified in the matrix, she has gone on to deliver new levels of leadership within her organization, and has done so with greater impact than would have ever been possible if she still had all those "weaknesses" hanging on her task list.

Awareness of the leadership principles we've been discussing, then, is not enough. To become a project leader, you will need to take proactive steps to build and cultivate these principles throughout the project, *and especially at the beginning of the project*. A true project leader will have mapped out a plan not only for the project, but also for how they will intentionally set up the moments that enable leadership when leadership matters most. Project managers must be intentional about their engagements with team members and create the moments that will enable them to become project leaders—not with grand gestures, like George C. Scott in front of the American flag in the movie *Patton*, but instead through small momentsduring the project. Becoming a project leader requires a daily commitment to serving the people on your team, your project's stakeholders, and your target audience. And by serving the people on your team, you will already be on your way to embracing the next approach: a focus on followership.

Focus on Followership

In some organizations, the notion of "leadership" is thought of as something that comes with a title. But when an organization or project is in crisis, what matters is not titles but the results that are produced by those who demonstrate leadership talents. To be sure, entitlements and labels do not make great leaders.

Any individual who aspires to become a true leader needs to understand the principles of leadership and be intentional about how they create the moments and relationships that build trust and perceptions. But as with many things in life, focusing on what you want *instead* of what it will take to get what you want, will inevitably lead to unsuccessful attempts. Clearly, project managers who want to become great project leaders should not focus on the attainment of titles. More to the point, they shouldn't even focus on "leadership"; instead, I would argue that they should focus on "followership."

Let me give you a couple of examples of the difference between leadership and followership. Kobe Bryant has on occasion scored fifty points or more in a basketball game. Gandhi spoke eloquently and persuasively about nonviolence. And Gene Krantz put all the smart engineers in one room when Apollo 13 had "a problem." However, without "followers"— those who agree to and perform the hard work the leader is asking them to do—the Lakers lose, India remains a colony, and Apollo 13 becomes a documentary without a heartwarming ending.

While the distinction between leadership and followership might only matter, or at the least only be witnessed, when projects are in crisis, an aspiring project leader should be thinking about cultivating followership starting on day one. In other words, the aspiring leader must focus on the needs and interests of the individuals that they want to inspire. To do so, the aspiring leader must put aside his or her needs and interests (aka "ego").

Each of the principles of leadership I've outlined in this chapter provide project managers with opportunities to create followership. In order to successfully *advocate a vision*, for example, the project leader must first tie the initiative's objectives with, or at least accommodate, the interests and goals of the individual team members—and to do that, the project leader will need to understand what those goals and interests are. Someone who is focused on followership will focus on creating their vision based on how it relates and inspires to the individuals on their team, and will be able to articulate what that connection is.

If one is *setting expectations* appropriately, meanwhile, they must be realistic about their team members' capabilities and competencies. Only by setting realistic expectations will project leaders be identified as having good judgment and a pragmatic understanding of what's possible. Sure, we should all have stretch goals, but most of us know what's 10% outside of our comfort zone and what's 100% outside of it, and the person who asks for and helps us achieve that additional 10% is someone we will follow.

Before followership can occur, a project leader must focus on *building trust*; they must do this from day one and continue through to the end of the project by being consistent and integral. Ensuring that individuals get to see a project leader demonstrating the core principles of trust—integrity, intent, capabilities, and results[32]—will facilitate the engendering of trust. Always "working behind the scenes," in contrast,

---

32. *Speed of Trust*, Stephen M. R. Covey, pg. 54

will hurt the development of followership. Just like math class, where you were rewarded for showing your work, a project leader will be entrusted with followership by their team when they openly demonstrate those core principles of trust.

Followership is also rooted in respect, and when a project leader can professionally *foster joint accountability*, the individuals on the team will respect that leader. By identifying when individuals are not keeping their commitments and then helping them recover and achieve their deliverables while maintaining professional courtesy (i.e., not humiliating or embarrassing anyone), a project leader gains the respect of their team. Of course, not all commitments can be met, but creating a culture of fear and punishment does not engender followership, only compliance. And when was the last time you felt allegiance to a leader who compelled you to feel compliant?

One of the best ways I've seen project leaders create a culture of accountability and followership is by *giving recognition—not just any recognition, but recognition* that is specific and tied to individuals' interests. It may seem counterintuitive that recognition would lead to people holding themselves more accountable, but in my experience this is absolutely the case. We all appreciate being acknowledged for our contributions in honest ways and in real terms, and when a project leader does this, they show that they are paying attention and they appreciate our efforts. We like the positive strokes, and since they can be rare, we tend to want to follow those people who give them.

The only constant in life is change, as cliché as that sounds, and the very nature of a project is to introduce change. In the case of planned changes—the desired outcomes of a project, for example—project leaders must *embrace change and effectively lead that change by applying principles of organizational change management. In the case of* unplanned change, project leaders must still *embrace change* rather than fight or deny it; the ability to resolve the issues causing these kinds of changes, and to marshal your troops to course-correct nimbly and ac-curately, is the perfect showcase for leadership talent.

Being a leader is not for the aggrandizement of the self but for the greater good of the team or organization. Sure, many of us crave the limelight and love the praise and recognition that comes with a job well done. Those are symbols of great individual achievements. Leadership, however, can never be the goal in and of itself, because to attain leader-ship requires a focus on the individuals on the team and achieving team results. By focusing on creating followership rather than the attainment of a leadership title, the aspiring project leader will put the interests of their team members, stakeholders, and users first, and in doing so will garner the trust, respect, and loyalty of those he or she serves.

PROFESSIONAL PROJECT LEADERSHIP: CONCLUSION

So that's project leadership in a nutshell: the seven principles (advo-cate a vision; engage the experts; set expectations; build trust; foster joint accountability; give recognition; and embrace change) and the two approaches (be intentional and focus on followership). Becoming a project leader does not happen overnight, and it is not easy—growth usually isn't. But if you apply these principles and approaches, it will become easier every time. In order to drive projects toward a more likely successful outcome, manage project commitments and stake-holder expectations, execute formal problem-solving when projects get knocked sideways by unforeseen circumstances, and achieve suc-cess at a better rate than the current 30–70% that project research points to, a project manager must perform at a higher level. By fol-lowing the above principles and having the right approach and inten-tion, you are more likely to perform and be perceived as a professional project leader.

KEY POINTS FOR CHAPTER 8:

● Professional project leadership is much more valuable than just performing Project Management well. It means *inspiring* and *motivating* other professionals into performing coordinated actions for a positive outcome. It represents a higher-caliber level of performance that ensures that no sponsor or stakeholder will ever question the value of your contribution. And it means the successful application of the art and science of Project Management and delivery upon the principles of commitment management.

● The goal of a leader is not to cultivate "leadership" but "followership"—the condition of being followed by others. In order to create followership, a project leader must be intentional about their actions and communications.

● Following the seven principles of professional project leadership will improve a project leader's odds of achieving followership. Those principles are: advocate a vision, engage the experts, set expectations, build trust, foster joint accountability, give recognition, and embrace change. Three of these are also on my Project Success Checklist—go figure.

CHAPTER 9

Checklist Item #6:

Minimize Scope & Requirements

"Nothing is more simple than greatness; indeed, to be simple is to be great."
—Ralph Waldo Emerson

Whether measured by schedule and budget, scope attainment, stakeholder expectation management, end user adoption, or market success, leading a project to a successful conclusion is challenging. What might be surprising to know is that sometimes the challenges are self-inflicted, and one of the leading causes of self-inflicted project failure is attempting to do too much. As I mentioned in Chapter 1, there are many studies on project success rates that illustrate how difficult project success can be. For instance, The Standish Group's 2009 study that found that only 32% of IT projects are "successful" (with success defined as being on schedule and on scope), with another 44% of projects ending up significantly over budget or schedule. Then there's IBM's 2008 *Global Making Change Work* study, which found that only 41% of change initiatives were successful. Combine that with "ambition" being one of the Project Management deadly sins as identified by The Standish

Group's *Top Five Reasons Why Projects Fail* presentation,[33] and perhaps the strong correlation between project failure and attempting to try to do too much becomes more apparent.

All projects are attempts to resolve a problem for a target audience. Too often, however, projects attempt to solve for too many symptoms of that problem, and therefore the scope of the project is needlessly too large. One of the pioneers of simplicity is Father William of Occam, best known for Occam's Razor, who once said, *"Entities must not be multiplied beyond necessity,"* (*I'll take 13th-century medieval philosophers for $500, Alex*). Sounds like Father Occam understood the problem with bloating your requirements list. Each additional piece of scope adds complexity and risk to a project, increasing its overall girth—an issue that may ultimately cause it to buckle and burst under its own weight.

The Standish Group can shed some light on this practice of trying to do too much with a project. A 2002 study they conducted, *Feature Usage on Typical Software Packages,* quantifies this self-inflicted problem: they found that 64% of features are rarely or never used, 13% are "often" used, and only 7% of features are "always" used. Hmm, the majority of the value is derived from 20% of the work; that sounds familiar, right?[34]

Now, I recognize that not all "rarely-used" or "never-used" features are "non-value-add" features. When I bought my last car, I placed value on the six airbags and the reinforced cage surrounding the passenger compartment, but I sure hope I never have to use them—and if I do, I will probably only use them once (i.e., "rarely"). That said, the Concatenate[35] feature in MS Excel is not the equivalent of an airbag that could save me from imprinting my facial features on my dashboard, and nobody is paying extra for MS Excel because of that feature. When I refer to "64% of features," I realize that this is a generalization and that there

---

33. "Top Ten Reasons Projects Succeed and The Five Reasons They Fail" keynote presentation by Jim Johnson, CEO of The Standish Group, at the January 2005 PMI Seminarworld in San Francisco.

34. The Pareto Principle states that 80% of the value of a thing comes from 20% of the work. The Standish Group's 2002 study, *Feature Usage of Typical Software Packages*, supports the Pareto Principle, as it found that 7% of features were used always and 13% of features were used often.

35. The Concatenate feature allows you to combine large amount of data from multiple cells into one cell within MS Excel.

are exceptions, but that doesn't change the fact that there are still a significant number of features being produced on our projects that do not add value to our end products.

So, if 64% of the features we're building add zero value for our users, and since every feature and requirement adds cost, time, complexity, and risk to a project, it is simply crazy to accept those 64% of features into your scope, right? Well, all you have to do to prevent this from happening on your projects is simply ask your stakeholders to identify the 64% of requirements that add zero value to the product and then remove them. Just kidding. *If only* it was that easy.

I'm sure every one of those features in the 64% category seemed like a great idea to someone on the teams that created the products the study looked at. That said, how do we identify those zero-value features? *By asking the right questions.* The concept of the 64% zero-value features and their inherent costs, complexities, and risks should lead the successful project manager to a logical extension of the claim in Occam's Razor—that *"simpler [solutions] are, other things being equal, generally better than more complex ones"*—or to go with the more colloquial "less is more" approach during requirements gathering.

> *"Everything should be made as simple as possible, but not simpler."*
>
> —Albert Einstein

The best way to identify that *"simpler solution"* is to first ask what the minimum amount of scope required to produce the desired result would be, and then to be ruthless in the pursuit of minimizing scope and requirements on your project. If you cannot prove that the feature is necessary in order to achieve an acceptable positive return on investment, then that requirement goes into a lower prioritization category and is not committed to or delivered in the first release.

"DO WE HAVE EVERYTHING WE NEED?"

How many times have you heard the question *"Do we have everything we need?"* while gathering project requirements? Be honest—how many times have you been the one asking it? This is the equivalent of the "Wafer-thin mint?" question posed in the Monty Python movie The Meaning of Life, and it has just as disastrous effects. It's an invitation to have your project "explode" down the road when the confluence of too many requirements and the exponential impact of cost, time, complexity, and risks leads to missed expectations. It also invariably produces the wise hindsight that comes up in the post-launch lessons learned session where you realize, maybe we attempted to do too much.

Therefore, instead of asking, *"do we have everything we need?"* I suggest you ask a different question—one with a much different intention and with better results.

HOW DO YOU EAT AN ELEPHANT?
ONE BITE AT A TIME.

Back in the Internet bubble version 1.0 days, I managed a project team that was, after a 50% reduction in force, was struggling with how to accomplish everything in our plans. We had identified all the reasons why it was impossible to accomplish all of the scope requirements, but as part of a scrappy start-up—one that just had shown half the employees the door—we didn't want to disappoint our sponsor.

When we presented our challenge and misguided options for getting all the work done to our sponsor, she laughed and said, "Of course you can't get all this done. I mean, hey, you do know how to eat an elephant, right?" The sponsor then went on to explain that attempting to bite off more than we could chew would doom us to failure. So she suggested an alternate course: "Let's roll up our sleeves," she said, "and determine what the minimal number of features we need for a marketable product." She then introduced another concept I still employ today:

"The question we need to ask," she told us, "is 'do we *need* everything we *have?*' not 'do we *have* everything we *need?*'"

Simple, beautiful, and spot-on. We then spent the next couple of hours crafting and debating the right feature list and the new requirements for our product. We didn't know about the Standish Group study about what a small percentage of features tend to be utilized, but our sponsor intuitively knew and embraced the concept. She knew that every requirement exponentially increases the amount of complexity, risks, time, and costs involved in a project and that any requirements that have a low level of impact on value (i.e., return on investment) should be deferred to a later release whenever possible.

Two months later, our first release nailed our acceptance criteria for launch; it was customer-ready. We had built a solid product that met all our requirements, we'd hit our schedule and budget, and we'd exceeded our stakeholders' expectations.

WHAT IF THE QUESTION IS NOT ENOUGH?

After I published my "Do we need everything we have?" story on the Slalom Consulting blog, I received a question about how to facilitate this process and eliminate the "64% non-value-add" features in more detail. In response, I provided the following steps from a recent requirements-gathering phase I had led that resulted in a number of requirements being de-prioritized, which felt like a "win" for the sponsor and stakeholders.

Feature Usage	Frequency
Always	7%
Often	13%
Sometimes	16%
Rarely	19%
Never	45%

Source: *Feature Usage on Typical Software, The Standish Group 2002*

I kicked off the first requirements-gathering meeting with a pie graph that illustrated the results of The Standish Group's 2002 *Feature Usage on Typical Software* study. This is a great conversation starter because nobody's baby is ugly, meaning that every stakeholder will initially defend the majority of their proposed requirements because they're sure they belong in the 7%, "always used" category. It is very interesting to note that the numbers in the study perfectly align with the Pareto Principle—which, as you may remember says that "80% of the value comes from 20% of the work." Keeping this in mind, let's go over the steps we took to "de-prioritize" a significant chunk of requirements. Notice I didn't say, "eliminate" or "cut"; that's because words matter, especially to the stakeholders whose pet requirements you are about to do away with. *De-prioritize* is a much easier word for them to wrap their minds around.

1) Force-Rank the Features

I'm a big fan of using weighted scorecards. A weighted scorecard is a tool that helps individuals and groups establish prioritized decision criteria before any options have been evaluated. Benefits of using a weighted scorecard include aligning on expectations of what is important in the decision and reducing or eliminating emotionality in the decision making process.[36] Here are the steps to creating a weighted scorecard:

1. Identify the criteria upon which the decision will be made. I like to try to limit these to four to six criteria elements (e.g., speed to market, ease of implementation, available resources, etc.).

2. Prioritize the criteria by giving each one a weight, with the total sum of the weights equaling 100.

---

36. My wife and I tried to use a weighted scorecard when buying our house, specifically to remove the emotionality out of the decision-making process. Have you ever bought a house? If so, you know it's nearly impossible to remove emotionality from the process, but the weighted scorecard when applied to home buying will at least indicate where your emotions are taking over your logic.

3. Develop a scoring system so there is an equal basis across all options when evaluating. I recommend a 1–5 scoring system (e.g., 1 = poor option, 3 = agreeable option, 5 = optimal option).

4. Start evaluating your options based on the criteria, giving scores and adding up the sum of scores for each option. If you are evaluating three options, the best choice will have the highest score.

5. Rip up the scorecard and go with the option you wanted in the first place (okay, that is intended as a joke. However, if your experience is like mine, both professionally and personally, this will likely happen as often as it does not).

The weighted scorecard, when combined with the business objectives, is a great way to objectively, and with full participation of the sponsor and key stakeholders, de-prioritize a lot of requirements—as long as the team is honest in their scoring assessments, that is.

2) Ask the End User

Hopefully, users were consulted during the original discovery and creation of requirements for your project. As discussed in Chapter 4, users are great at describing pain points and quantifying the value of a solution, and even though they are not always so great at identifying solutions, they can tell you what they like and don't like. The litmus test for any requirement or feature should be to ask, "Does it contribute to solving the users' problem?" If not, it should be given lower priority. I'm always surprised at how many requirements will fall out at this phase. And keep in mind that this data or evidence can be collected very quickly. You can always ask your stakeholders to come prepared with this kind of data to the requirements-gathering sessions. In my example, we had representatives of the users in the process, so we were able to ask them directly how they felt about each of the proposed requirements, and thankfully these were brutally honest people.

3) Prototype Options

For those requirements that are on the borderline between being in scope and de-prioritized, one way to help inform the decision is to prototype the requirements, either on paper or in another similar, simple format, and then ask a small number of users for feedback. This allows your customers to provide feedback, and that information can be used between you and the stakeholders to determine if that requirement will be in scope or not. Jakob Nielsen, the UI and Web guru, once wrote that while large sample-sized usability studies are great for academics, he got the same value from asking five people for their opinions as he did when he surveyed 1,000.[37]

4) Let the Metrics Speak

Using Rough Order of Magnitude estimates,[38] you can quickly identify differences between options based on their alignment with value creation and the relative costs associated with developing them. Requirements can also be measured by complexity and risk estimates, making the simpler solution even more apparent and attractive.

After performing these steps, we were successfully able to get our requirements list down to what all team members and stakeholders thought was a good, concise list—one that would enable rapid development and deployment of the product, and would leave us the opportunity to add features in later phases.

---

37. *Designing Web Usability* was one of those web designer bibles of a book that I saw on so many bookshelves during the Internet bubble. What I enjoyed about the book was that it dripped of common sense time and time again. Even the idea that asking five people was just as effective as asking 1,000 was brilliant; a lot of requirement discussions can be short-circuited once five people say "no way."
38. A Rough Order of Magnitude or ROM estimate translates to "pulling the data out of your hat" based on heuristics, which is another pseudo-scientific word for "rule of thumb."

AGILE METHODOLOGY EMBRACES THE SIMPLER SOLUTION

Another approach to rapid development is using one of the Agile development methodologies, such as Scrum or XP, which, when performed correctly, attempts to build only that which adds value. Although I've never actually heard anyone else argue this, from my experience the delivery of a "simpler solution" is one of the primary benefits of the Agile methodology. Rather than the all-you-can-eat approach witnessed in projects that follow the waterfall methodology, an Agile project will start with the "minimum viable product" feature list and incrementally build a shippable product. Doing this makes it more likely that a product owner will say, "This is good enough to give to customers"—even when there are many more features identified and yet to be built. The second primary benefit of Agile from my perspective is that due to the nature of the 2-4 week iterations, every day is treated as valuable as the next by the team, as opposed to on a project following the waterfall methodology, where the first week is less productive than the last week before a launch.

In my experience on a waterfall project, product owners are more likely to attempt to cram additional features into the requirements because 1) they may think it will be a long time before the users see the final product, and 2) cost and time are the key (only?) forcing functions for limiting scope and requirements. This is not a mentality that embraces the "simpler solution." The waterfall method is a much more top-down model, whereas Agile builds from the bottom up and attempts to produce that discernible "simpler solution" and bare-minimum feature set sooner. That is the intention of Agile; when it is put into action, of course, your experience may vary.

Using an iterative development methodology allows you to adjust to complexity and change better, and determine which features your customer values the most. By developing the most important features and embedding a process that allows greater flexibility for change and complexity, when done well, Agile will allow you to ship a product and achieve project objectives faster than the applying a traditional, waterfall methodology. Most Agile proponents I know do not agree that Agile "is faster," and when comparing original estimates and project schedules during the planning phase, duration may look the same. What I am stating is that Agile affords the team the opportunity to ship earlier than planned because they get to a validated valuable product sooner, whereas Waterfall projects are rarely early (never heard of one myself) because you are supposed to build everything, test everything, fix everything, re-test everything, and ship everything.

I have always taken this "path of least resistance" approach to projects, and have intentionally chosen to do the least amount of work required in order to attain the desired objectives. And it's not because I'm lazy, but because it is more efficient and it allows for bandwidth to deal with the things that go as unplanned. I embrace the "least work possible" approach because I've discovered that each additional piece of scope not only adds more time and cost, but also exponentially increases the amount of complexity and risk. When additional work is identified with questionable or no clear benefits, this is an invitation to chaos and failure. With the time and energy I save by forcing the "simpler solution," I allow myself more bandwidth to prepare for the inevitable unknown that I know from experience will be knocking on my door soon enough.

MINIMIZE SCOPE & REQUIREMENTS: CONCLUSION

If you have ever packed the car for a road trip with kids, the "Do we need everything we have?" question should be very familiar. The road trip is a great analogy for minimizing scope and requirements, because of the fixed constraints of space and the goal of having satisfied stakeholders (or a desire to avoid unhappy stakeholders). And just like explaining to a four-year-old why he can't bring his three-foot-tall stuffed animal along for the trip, the conversation with sponsors and stakeholders might be a little surreal at times. The successful project manager will know that driving toward a "simpler solution" will more likely contribute to success than an "all aboard" approach. And yes, the promise of ice cream after a long journey can work well in both cases.

It's not just the promise of ice cream that should make you lean towards simpler solutions—much stronger minds than mine have identified that simpler solutions are better solutions. If Ralph Waldo Emerson, Albert Einstein, and Father Occam are all embracing simplicity as a guiding principle, maybe there's something to it.

KEY POINTS FOR CHAPTER 9:

- Simple solutions are better than complex ones, although it's harder to develop simpler solutions, which is one reason why people tend to stop at the complex ones.

- Each additional requirement and piece of scope on your project not only adds time and cost, but also to risk and complexity. To fail to be judicious about the acceptance of each requirement and piece of scope is to court problems and possible failure.

- "Do we need everything we have?" is a great way to question assumptions about project requirements and scope and to start the conversation about reducing the amount of work required to deliver desired outcomes.

CHAPTER 10

Checklist Item #7:

Proactive Risk Management

Most of what's written about Risk Management is firmly rooted in the *science* of Project Management; how to calculate risk factors, the four types of risk responses, the thresholds for risk severity, and so on. These are all important, for they provide the basis for the "what" of Risk Management. However, I want to spend some time focusing on the social skills required for the "how"—the *art*—of Risk Management, since it is a major contributing factor to a successful project. Before we get to the "how" of Risk Management, however, let's get clear on the "why"— specifically, the value Risk Management contributes to successful projects.

RISK MANAGEMENT, PART 1:
THE VALUE OF RISK MANAGEMENT

"If you are looking for perfect safety, you will do well to sit on a fence and watch the birds; but if you really wish to learn, you must mount a machine and become acquainted with its tricks by actual trial."

—Wilbur Wright[39]

---

39. Wilbur Wright's address to the Western Society of Engineers in Chicago, September 18, 1901.

Any endeavor of significance comes with the potential for great reward; as the saying goes, the greater the reward, the greater the risks. Maybe I have that backwards, but to paraphrase Wilbur Wright, there is a limited amount to gain from sitting on the sidelines. It's interesting to note that risk tolerance, or the willingness to take risks, tends to be higher at the beginning of a project than in the middle. Recently I was reading about newly discovered and costly problems on a major bridge project underway here in the Seattle area, and in response to questions about the decision-making that lead to the problems, Paula Hammond, the Washington State Transportation Secretary, was quoted as saying: "Everybody wants you to take risks until something goes wrong."[40]

This is an incredibly telling quote—not only because it's true, but because it provides a glimpse into the pressures placed on project leaders at the beginning of projects to be more aggressive with scope, schedule, and budget—in other words, to have a high tolerance for risk—right up until something goes wrong.

However, the risk versus rewards equation (plus the added pressure of a higher risk tolerance at the beginning of a project) does not mean that you are powerless when it comes to tipping the odds of delivering the rewards in your favor. In fact, that is exactly what Proactive Risk Management does for you. As I've said many times already now, *all projects will be knocked sideways at some point*. Guaranteed. It is an immutable law of Project Management. Saying "all projects will go sideways" is as sure as saying "there's chance of rain" when you're a weather forecaster in Seattle.

Problems don't only occur on those projects where project managers have employed ineffective or lazy Risk Management practices—or bad Project Management in general—although that will make such problems more likely, for sure. Some of the most challenged projects I've seen have had some of the best Risk Management talents I've ever known. But it's been my experience that the more senior and more talented the project manager, the more likely they are to be assigned to a

40. *"State admits costly mistakes on 520 bridge"* The Seattle Times, February 26, 2013

project with higher risk and complexity, which means that the project is even more likely to go sideways. If you don't buy that, we should talk with our Project Management friends on the 787 project at Boeing, or those who were on the Space Shuttle program at NASA. Those Boeing and NASA project managers are extremely talented and experienced, yet those projects have had their share of very public challenges and failures. And those challenges are definitely not due to a lack of professional Risk Management—those projects were simply more difficult.

I say that every project will be knocked sideways at some point because I haven't met a project manager or been on a project that didn't experience that "Houston, we have a problem" moment. In every project management presentation I give, I ask my audience members to raise their hand if they have ever been on a project over three weeks in duration that did not have some serious, unforeseen challenge knock the project sideways. In five years of doing this, I have not had one project manager keep their hand down.

"Anticipate the difficult by managing the easy."
—Lao Tsu

In my experience, the value of Proactive Risk Management is to *specifically* identify and plan for all the items that may knock the project sideways so you have the personal bandwidth to deal with unforeseen challenges when they come along. Now that you know something is coming, let's talk about what you can do to prepare for when those knowable risks become actual issues.

"There are known knowns; there are things we know that we know. There are known unknowns; that is to say, there are things that we now know we don't know. But there are also unknown unknowns—there are things we do not know we don't know."
—Donald Rumsfeld, United States Secretary of Defense, 2002

In this chapter, I will urge you to perform a proactive style of Risk Management as project manager—identifying and assessing all "known unknown" items so that when that "unknown unknown"[41] event does occur, you have the personal bandwidth to detect the trigger event and marshal your troops to triage and respond quickly and appropriately. In this chapter, I'll explain exactly what Proactive Risk Management is, and then I will share some of the risk identification and risk assessment practices I have found great value in performing on my projects.

PROACTIVE RISK MANAGEMENT

Far too often in my career, I have witnessed two types of Risk Management that do very little to keep a project from going off the rails. I'll categorize the first type as "nice start" Risk Management, and the second as "sky is falling" Risk Management. With "nice start" Risk Management, detailed plans are made for how risks will be managed at the beginning of the project, and then a long list of risks are identified, assessed, and categorized appropriately. All the right things done in the right order. Then the real work starts, and the Risk Management plan gets left on some shared drive on the corporate network, collecting dust. It's like that last piece of chocolate in the assortment box—it looks good from the outside, but then you bite into it and it's filled with some obnoxious flavor. The second type of ineffective Risk Management, "sky is falling" Risk Management, no plan is developed nor are risks identified and triaged early on. Instead, risks are identified in real time and they are all treated the same, regardless of their potential impact upon the project. To be clear, Proactive Risk Management is neither of the above.

Proactive Risk Management is complete, powerful, valuable—and yes, takes a more upfront planning and ongoing maintenance than "nice start" and "sky is falling," however the results are more effective for the

---

41. Risks are also referred to as "known unknowns" and "unknown unknowns." "Known unknowns" and "unknown unknowns" entered pop culture when, in 2002, US Secretary of Defense Donald Rumsfeld made what some called a "clumsy" attempt to explain the complexities of the war in Iraq. Most of us who are familiar with Project Management, however, were completely following along with Mr. Rumsfeld's description of risks.

successful management and addressing of risks. Proactive Risk Management a combination of attitude and approach:

- *Attitude*—Taking Risk Management very seriously in order to protect personal and team bandwidth for when the big, unforeseen problems occur.

- *Approach*—Setting up appropriate and sustainable Risk Management processes that reasonably safeguard the project baselines and ensure personal and team bandwidth for dealing with the unknown unknown.

Another way to think about this is project insurance: the project is paying up front to protect your team's ability to identify and address big issues—which, in turn, will hopefully result in delivery of value throughout project execution. So, where does that start? With a Risk Management Plan.

Risk Management Plan

Your Risk Management Plan outlines how risks will be managed throughout the life of your project. It should include:

- The basics of the process: how risks will be identified and assessed

- How risks will be monitored and communicated

- How time and cost contingencies will be calculated and included in the project schedule and budget

The plan will need to be reviewed and approved by the project sponsor, the project leads, and possibly the project steering committee. Getting sign-off from these different parties will show that your primary stakeholders approve of how you plan to manage those risks, and give you assurance that they will participate in the process as outlined in the plan. It will also help you set expectations with your stakeholders. Pretty straightforward, right? What's not entirely straightforward, however— but is a crucial part of the plan—is how you are going to handle your contingency reserve.

CONTINGENCY

Since the word "contingency" can sometimes be misunderstood, I want to take a moment to clarify what I mean when I use this term. Contingency is not "buffer" or "fluff" added to the budget or schedule based on the theory that "stuff happens." And contingency is not meant to be spent on change controls.[42] Spending contingency dollars on a change means decreasing your ability to minimize the impact when a risk is realized.

To call contingency a "buffer" indicates a lack of understanding of its value and purpose, and like a shark with blood in the water, some stakeholders will chew up that line item in the project budget because they see it either as sandbagging by the project team or because they feel it's money left on the table—money that can pay for one or more of those features they had to de-prioritize when you were minimizing scope and requirements.

So, contingency is not a buffer; it is a schedule and budget resource pool dedicated to reducing the impact to project baselines when a risk is realized. The contingency for budget is commonly referred to as a contingency reserve; the contingency for time is usually referred to as a schedule contingency. And yes, technically, I'd agree that contingency is part of the science of Project Management; I know I said I wouldn't be

---

42. A change control item is a "change" to one or more approved baselines, which means the project needs more time and/or money to accommodate the change.

talking about the science, so let me just say that the art of contingency comes in knowing its value to projects and making sure it is part of your Project Management practice.

Before we get into the differences between budgeting and scheduling contingency, let's first discuss how contingency is calculated. One starts by analyzing all identified risks; then you determine the probability of each of those risks being realized, as well as what the impact will be if that happens (impact is measured in dollars for contingency reserve, and days for schedule contingency). When you multiply the probability and impact, you get the risk factor for each individual risk. For instance, let's say there is a risk that a key resource will not be available for the project: for the contingency reserve, the impact will be that you'll have to obtain a contractor for two months at the cost of $50K. If the probability of the key resource not being available is 50%, then you multiply the cost ($50K) by that probability (50%), resulting in a risk score of $25K.

The sum of all the risk scores you calculate should be used to inform the size of your project's contingency. That sum will cover the entire risk profile for your project, and should not be thought of as a collection of individual insurance plans for specific deliverables or phases. In other words, if the sum of your risk factors in the design phase is $5K and ten days, and none of the risks you foresaw occur during that phase, you should not give that contingency back to the project for other uses—instead, that amount should be carried forward as contingency for the rest of the project. This is because the risk scores are based on a fraction of the actual impact of a risk occurring; in the above example, for instance, a testing phase risk might have an actual impact of $50K and twenty days, but let's say you set the risk score at $5K and two days because the probability of the risk being realized was set at 10%. That design phase contingency of $5K and ten days sure will be handy later when that testing risk rears its ugly head, right?

Also, notice that I said in the last paragraph that the sum of risk scores should "inform" the size of the contingency, not "determine" the size of the reserve. This is where you will need to apply that art of Project Management and use your judgment to recommend how much to set aside for your contingency. Some organizations will use a blanket 10% of approved budget and schedule for contingency. If your organization uses this same practice, my suggestion is to calculate your contingency using the sum of risk factors and determine which one is higher. If 10% is higher, then safeguard the amount you need for schedule and budget contingencies and allow stakeholders to chip away at the delta between the 10% and the amount you are managing as contingency. If your contingency is greater than the 10%, then start building your case for requesting a larger schedule or budget contingency—I'd recommend starting your formal request by asking each member of the approval committee if they have ever been on a project where something unforeseen did not knock them sideways.

Contingency Type 1: Contingency Reserve

"Contingency reserve" refers to the amount of money set aside for budgetary impacts of risks occurring during a project. When calculating the budget risk scores, multiply probability and impact in dollar amounts. The sum of the risk scores should be used to inform the size of the contingency reserve. Depending on the level of maturity of one's organization, the practice of maintaining a contingency reserve as part of the project finances will vary. The existence of a contingency reserve is basically an adherence to that immutable Project Management law that unexpected things—both large and small—will inevitably occur on the project, and if you don't have a budget reserve set aside, you will have to adjust your budget—usually at the expense of other planned projects, or maybe even the quality of your end product.

Contingency Type 2: Schedule Contingency

Just as a contingency reserve helps to minimize the impact of known unknowns upon cost, a schedule contingency helps to minimize their impact upon time. Measured in days instead of dollars, the schedule contingency ensures that stakeholder expectations for the project schedule includes accommodations for the occurrence of those known and unknown unknowns. When calculating the schedule risk scores, then, you multiply probability and impact in days. Then you can use the sum of the risk score to inform the size of your schedule contingency.

There are two significant, and somewhat conflicting, considerations that you will need to contemplate when applying schedule contingency, and both are rooted in the art of Project Management. The first is how to apply schedule contingency to your project plan; the second is the impact that the application of schedule contingency may have on your team. When applying schedule contingency to your project plan, do not place one line item in between "Signoff" and "Launch" with the total number of days set aside as your schedule contingency; doing so will misrepresent when your project will actually need the insurance which the contingency provides. Sure, the net effect might be the same—but you may be setting the wrong expectations for all other milestones in the project plan, and remember, it's all about setting, managing, and delivering on expectations. That said, my recommendation is to divide the schedule contingency into the appropriate phases or deliverables as determined by the risks attached to each one. For instance, if there is a risk associated with a design deliverable, it makes a lot more sense to put that part of the schedule contingency into the design phase—that way, if the risk materializes, you'll have extra days built in to deal with it, and future milestone dates won't be affected.

Now that you have distributed your schedule contingency smartly throughout your project plan, I give you two words of caution: Parkinson's Law.[43] Parkinson's Law states that work will grow and shrink based on the amount of time that is given. I refer to this principle as the "college term paper" syndrome. Maybe you've had this experience: the instructor assigns a term paper on the first day of class, but no one starts working on the assignment until the week before it's due, and then there's the "all-nighter" the evening before the due date where the majority of the work happens. How this applies to schedule contingency is that when team members see that there is, for example, a week of schedule contingency time inserted into the project plan before a major deliverable or milestone date, they might be tempted to take that time to complete that specific work. Parkinson's Law would suggest that the quality of work might not increase during that "extra" time, and the cost to the project is that you're losing the schedule contingency time for a later risk that does occur.

To combat Parkinson's Law having an impact on my Schedule Contingency, I like to tell my teams that contingency is another way of saying their "nights and weekends"—as in, if you eat into schedule contingency now, when you don't have to, you will likely be working on nights and weekends later in the project.

Contingency reserve and schedule contingency are major pieces of proactive risk management because they allow you to focus on the issue while minimizing the impact of the issue, literally buying the project time to recover. In doing so, you are better able to set and manage stakeholder expectations from the beginning of the project, starting with the very first discussion about contingency and have a plan for managing risks and issues: "Read my lips: bad stuff will happen. Here's how we are going to deal with it." The successful project manager will never refer to contingency as "buffer" or "fluff," because, as we've just gone over, that just courts problems for the project manager.

---

43. Parkinson's Law runs counter to my "Benefits of Procrastination" theory, however, Parkinson's Law is on Wikipedia and my theory only exists in these pages, my presentations, and sometimes in my actions. To read more on Parkinson's Law, go to: http://en.wikipedia.org/wiki/Parkinson%27s_law

Contingency Best Practices

I was working on a client project a few years ago where each project manager on the client's team had a different understanding of what contingency was meant to be used for and how it should be calculated. Some projects used contingency for change requests (which should actually come from another budgetary reserve called a "management reserve"), whereas other projects used it for bad estimates. The organization had a standard definition for contingency—but unfortunately, it was clear as mud and was therefore subject to interpretation.

I worked with my Project Management colleagues to agree to a single definition and protocol, and then we worked with our sponsors to socialize and gain agreement on the process. We set the minimum threshold of contingency at 10% of schedule and budget, with the caveat that project managers could also submit estimates for schedule and budget, as long as the risk calculations were validated and signed off on by the sponsors. The new process helped establish greater transparency and predictability, which in turn led to greater credibility for the project managers. This new definition and process was shared with the larger organization and has now become a standard practice for the company.

When helping clients establish contingency best practices, I have them do the following:

1. Agree on the definition of schedule contingency and contingency reserve

2. Determine how to calculate contingency

3. Define additional contingency procedures, such as:

   - What to do when new risks are identified that increase the risk profile and subsequently require larger contingencies.

- If/when to release contingency dollars and days back to the portfolio as risk trigger events pass, or decide how to spend unused reserve.

Defining contingency for schedule and budget in this way provides greater transparency, predictability, and credibility to stakeholders—and those seem like three pretty good objectives for project managers in everything they do, don't they?

PROACTIVE RISK MANAGEMENT SUMMARY

One of my favorite examples of Proactive Risk Management is the Zombie Preparedness blog on the Center for Disease Control's (CDC's) website.[44] Since pop culture has been enthralled with the "impending" zombie apocalypse, the CDC has jumped on the bandwagon by incorporating plans for dealing with a zombie apocalypse much as they suggest preparations for hurricanes, earthquakes, and other natural disasters. Now, I'm sure no one at the CDC truly believes the risk is real or imminent, but as Dr. Ali Khan of the CDC writes:

> *"So what do you need to do before zombies . . . or hurricanes or pandemics, for example, actually happen? First of all, you should have an emergency kit in your house. This includes things like water, food, and other supplies to get you through the first couple of days before you can locate a zombie-free refugee camp (or in the event of a natural disaster,[45] it will buy you some time until you are able to make your way to an evacuation shelter or utility lines are restored)."*

---

44. No joke, the CDC has a Zombie Apocalypse Preparedness blog on its website, which can be found at http://blogs.cdc.gov/publichealthmatters/category/zombies

45. For a more information from the CDC about other natural disasters, please go to http://emergency.cdc.gov/disasters/

In order to mitigate the risk of thousands of Americans not being prepared when a real disaster strikes, the CDC has embraced the zombie apocalypse craze in order to get its message of preparedness out to millions of people who are pointed to their site out of a sense of humor. The risk of a zombie pandemic is small, but the CDC knows that thousands, if not millions, will be impacted each year by natural disasters, and their message of preparedness has reached a larger audience because of this tactic.

Proactive Risk Management is a key process that leads to successful projects. Because all projects will be challenged at some point, Proactive Risk Management will enable the successful project manager to safeguard their bandwidth to deal with the big, unforeseen issues that knock the project sideways. Contingency is a major piece of Proactive Risk Management because it enables project managers to minimize the impact when something goes wrong, and literally buys the project time to recover.

Now, let's discuss where the Risk Management rubber meets the road: the identification of risks. I've got a process that doubles as a risk identifier and a means of gaining team consensus on whether a project is feasible. Let's take a look.

RISK MANAGEMENT, PART 2: RISK IDENTIFICATION

Risk identification is a very straightforward process in which you and your team identify project risk. Usually this process takes place in a conference room where the project manager asks team members to identify project risks and typically many risks are identified. It's a very exciting process.

Okay, as described above, the process is *not* exciting. Where the excitement does come from, however, is when the risks you've identified don't feel like all the true risks that exist for the project. Sometimes this happens because people are afraid to look like naysayers. Sometimes it's because team members are risk-tolerant and don't identify risks because "they'll be dealt with *if* they occur." But the biggest threat that might be occurring when risks are not being identified is that a team member, or the entire team, may not feel like the project goals are attainable. When this happens, your team may not be that interested in identifying the small things that may not matter. You could compare this, for instance, to rearranging the deck chairs on the Titanic.

That sinking feeling is a huge risk to the success of your project, and it needs to be addressed. Regardless of whether your team members' perceptions are based in reality or are unfounded, you will want to focus on discovering those concerns about feasibility and success immediately.

"Why Won't This Work?"

If you are working with a team that you believe is not fully participating in the Risk Identification process, or if you perceive that there's a larger concern about project feasibility, instead of sounding like the teacher in the movie *Ferris Bueller's Day Off*—droning on and taking role call ("*Buel-ler? Buel-ler?*")[46]—you will need to change tack and create a new way to discover the underlying issues.

One of the best ways I know of to combat lack of participation or negative perceptions of project feasibility is to conduct what's called a "*Why won't this work?*" meeting. The purpose of this type of meeting is to facilitate a conversation with all team members about all the reasons why the project may fail. There is a distinct difference between a *risk* and a *cause for failure*, and this has a visceral effect on participants. A risk means the project has a likelihood of succeeding—but if you're fixated on thinking the project is doomed, then "risks" are trivial. The "Why won't this work?" process combines the Risk Management phases of risk

---

46. Not my favorite '80s teenager movie (I'm a *Breakfast Club* man myself), *Ferris Bueller's Day Off* is a classic tale of three teenagers enjoying the last of their salad days before entering adulthood/college. For more on the movie, check out: http://en.wikipedia.org/wiki/Ferris_bueller

identification, risk assessment, and risk response, and can even be used when team participation or overall project feasibility is not an issue. Below are the steps I use to conduct the meeting.

First, kick off the meeting by sharing with the team your perceptions of any underlying factors that put the project success at jeopardy. Ask the team to help identify any reasons *why it may not work* (hence the name of the meeting). Then ask the meeting participants to go around the room and offer reasons they identify where failure may be possible.

Once you have captured all the possible reasons for failure on the whiteboard, start triaging which ideas should be analyzed first by asking, "Which of these potential issues have either a high, medium, or low likelihood of occurring, and which ones will have a major or minor impact to the project if they do occur?" This is a great way to engage the participants in a dialogue about the prioritization of the items, which will in turn lead to:

a) the sharing of knowledge of why a failure reason is not valid—usually someone will have information that the identifying person did not

b) the elimination of the random "volcano eruption" or "local sports team makes the playoffs" prognostications. And sadly, yes, I have seen both events identified as risks on projects.

With that shortened and prioritized list, you can now start to address the remaining items and ask, "What can we do to prevent these from happening or to mitigate the impact of each one if they do happen?" This will demonstrate to team members in the room which of the risks require response planning and which require monitoring—your normal risk response steps. But more importantly, by asking both questions—*"Why won't this work?"* and *"What can we do?"*—the team will accomplish several things in addition to risk identification, including:

- *Empowerment*—The project manager is setting the tone early in the project that they want to hear from everyone on any concern that they may have. Again, the goal is to identify all the "known unknowns" so you have the bandwidth to detect and deal with the "unknown unknowns" that appear in midflight and knock the project sideways. If the project is knocked sideways by something that was actually known by a project team member but not shared, the project manager may have not empowered the team member to announce the foreseeable problem.

- *Consensus*—Are the project goals achievable? This meeting will result in the team agreeing either yes or no, and the successful project manager will want to know this before getting too far into the project.

Of all the reasons to hold this meeting, the most important in my opinion is consensus. The result of the meeting should point to whether most team members think the project is achievable or not. Hopefully, even though this dialogue is focused on creating a significant list of potential risks, it will make your team members feel like those items can be addressed appropriately and the project can be successful

Conversely, if your team arrives at the consensus that the project is not doable after a "Why won't this work?" meeting, then you will need to start focusing all efforts immediately on addressing this concern. A lack of belief in success will result in poor quality, missed deadlines, and bad morale. This would be a great time to recruit the sponsor and key stakeholders to get involved with addressing the team's, and now your, concerns about failure. Possible options for the sponsor and key stakeholders to consider are potential changes to scope, finding a direction more aligned with what is feasible, and/or becoming closely involved in addressing the potential morale issues that may impact project performance.

Real-World Experience

The most valuable time I facilitated a "Why won't this work?" meeting was not at the beginning of a project, as I prescribed above, but when I was assigned to a project midflight. The reason I held this meeting was because after the first several discussions I had with project team members, each conversation would end with, "*Oh yeah, and this project is doomed.*"

"*What?*" I responded as intelligently as possible, and followed up that bit of genius by asking, "*Why?*" Each reason I heard was followed by another. I would ask if any of these issues had been discussed by the team, and the common response was, "*No one asked.*" So I scheduled the meeting.

At the "*Why won't this work?*" meeting, I handed out sticky notes and asked each person to write down their reasons why the project would most likely fail. I went around and collected the sticky notes as they were written, then stuck each one on the whiteboard. When the group was done writing, I read each sticky note and asked for three things: a description of the reason; an explanation of whether there was any evidence of the reason actually occurring (or the probability of the reason actually occurring); and an assessment of the total impact of the reason. I was prioritizing, in other words, by asking for probability and severity. Then I asked something that went against normal brainstorming rules: I asked the group to argue why the reason was not a valid one. Some of the dire risks were actually "resolved" right there, and it was because the person who identified the risk was missing some critical information that another person in the room had. There were a couple reasons that the team agreed were true risks to the project, and we discussed and identified ways to mitigate the impact of those risks if they were realized at any point. Then I asked one more question: "*Knowing what you now know, who here thinks the project will be successful?*" Talk about risky. What if only half the room had raised their hand? What if there were no raised hands? Technically speaking, that would have been "a bummer."

Fortunately, everyone raised their hand—some more quickly than others, but everyone did. The lesson was that if we collaborate, share information, and work together, we can achieve the goals of the project. That was powerful. The team did a 180-degree turn on their prognosis of the project, and four months later we had a successful launch.

RISK IDENTIFICATION SUMMARY

Identifying risks is one of the first steps in the Risk Management process. The "*Why won't this work?*" meeting is both a great way to identify risks and a meaningful collaboration process to gain consensus through teamwork and make a statement about the feasibility of a project. In facilitating this conversation, the successful project manager will start the Risk Management process by identifying most of the known risks, a process that should uncover any significant morale issues, and also enable the project manager to be perceived by the team as a true leader. Not bad outcomes for just one meeting.

Since not all risks are created equally, they should not be treated as such. Unfortunately, there are projects where stakeholders treat all identified risks at DEFCON 1 levels.[47] That's unreasonable—it's a waste of time, energy, and money—and the successful project manager won't let that happen.

---

47. The United States Armed Forces uses the Defense Readiness Condition, or DEFCON, to indicate current threat levels to the national security of the country. DEFCON 1 indicates the most severe stage.

RISK MANAGEMENT, PART 3:
RISK ASSESSMENT

Risk assessment is what they do in the movies when they discover that an asteroid is careening towards Earth: they determine the probability and severity of an impact, and then they shove Bruce Willis into a rocket ship. Ground Control to Major Chicken Little (with apologies to David Bowie).

Since not all risks are created equally, they should not be treated as such. In other words, this should not be like the movie *Armageddon*, it should be more like George Orwell's *Animal Farm*: two legs good, four legs bad. In other words, in performing Risk Assessment, you can rank the risks efficiently—ensuring that the team's focus is on what's important and deserving of the team's attention—and not react as if the sky is falling every time someone sneezes up a new risk (Bird flu, anyone?!). How do you do this? It's all in the risk assessment process, which includes triaging the impact and probability of the risk, then determining the appropriate response to each risk. By doing the assessment early and before the risk is realized, you will allow your team time to come up with clear-headed alternatives. A risk on paper is a lot less scary than one that is blocking out the sun.

Not All Risks Are Negative

"Did I just blow your mind?"
                    —Ricky Bobby[48]

That's right, there are risks that have a positive impact upon a project. The definition of a risk is "an uncertain event or condition that, if occurs, has a positive or negative effect on a project's objectives."[49] Examples may include:

48. Quote from the main character in the Will Ferrell movie *Talladega Nights: The Ballad of Ricky Bobby*. For more information, go to: http://en.wikipedia.org/wiki/Ricky_bobby
49. *A Guide to the Project Management Body of Knowledge*, Project Management Institute, pg. 207

- Tasks not taking as long as estimated

- Less resources are needed to accomplish a deliverable than expected

- Another project delivers functionality that can be repurposed

These are all real-life examples of positive risks I've witnessed on projects that resulted in favorable variances to project baselines.

If the nirvana of Project Management is all about increasing predictability in setting and managing project expectations, then you should incorporate positive and negative risks in your risk management plans, which may also impact your contingencies. So let's discuss how to assess *all* risks, both positive and negative.

Not All Risks Should Be Treated The Same

Some identified risks are more likely to occur than others, and some, if realized, would have a bigger impact than others. Intuitively, this should make sense. But when faced with a long list of risks, I've seen teams (and their leaders) have two reactions that sound like they're from the Aesop's vault of unreleased fables—a story I would call "*The Ostrich and the Chicken.*"

The ostrich represents those who collectively put their heads in the sand, ignoring the risks and hoping they don't occur. *The chicken*—as in, "Chicken Little"—represents those who run around treating any identified risk as a major threat to the health of the project and expending a disproportionate amount of time and effort to plan for and address the outcome those potential events. In my experience, the chicken's over-reactive behavior can actually cause people to resort to ostrich behavior—mostly as a way to avoid future chicken panic attacks. In both cases, the reactions are caused by a feeling of being overwhelmed by the list of risks and an inability to rank and categorize said risks. In the case of the *chicken*, the project usually encounters an unintended consequence of a badly run risk management process: team members do not identify or communicate new risks due to an extreme reaction to all previously identified risks.

So how can you appropriately assess risks and create a sense of ranking or categorization amongst the list of risks? Well, first let's go back to the basic premise that some risks are more likely to occur and some will have a bigger impact if and when they do occur. If that is the case, then why not use probability and impact as the two dimensions for ranking risks?

Building on that idea, let's take a quick quiz. Which of the following risks do you think a project manager should focus on first?

- A risk with a $1M impact and a 10% probability of occurring?

- A risk with a $200K impact and an 80% probability of occurring?

- A risk with a $10K impact and 90% probability of occurring?

All three might seem like significant risks—however, even though the first risk has the biggest impact, $1M, the second one is more deserving of attention because of the impact *and* the probability. Let me tell you why: because the risk score is bigger in the second scenario.

RISK SCORES

As we discussed in Part 1 of this chapter, when you identify the probability and impact of each risk, you can take those two factors and multiply them together to generate a risk score. In doing so, the risks can easily be ranked and ordered, allowing for the team and sponsors to dialogue about how to respond to each risk.

In the above example, here are the Risk Scores:

- Risk #1: $1M impact x 10% probability = $100K Risk Score

- Risk #2: $200K impact x 80% probability = $160K Risk Score

- Risk #3: $10K impact x 90% probability = $9K Risk Score

Given these results, the second risk clearly represents a bigger threat to the project's baselines.

The risk score helps us determine a sense of priority amongst the risks. And based on that prioritization, you can determine what type of response should be assigned to the various risk levels.

RISK RESPONSE

The risk score will help in the prioritization of risks, which in turn will help you determine the appropriate risk response to engage in. There are five types of responses, and they are:

- *Addressing the risk*—incorporating specific plans into the project scope to deal with the high level of impact or probability that the risk will occur

- *Mitigating the risk*—developing plans to resolve the risk if the risk occurs

- *Avoiding the risk*—removing scope that includes risk from the project

- *Transferring the risk*—transferring ownership of scope to another party so they now are accountable for the risk and subsequent consequences

- *Accepting the risk*—doing nothing, but monitoring the risk triggers so you'll know if the risk occurs and have the opportunity to develop and implement plans to address it

To determine which responses are appropriate for which risks, you should lead a discussion with your team and stakeholders where responses are aligned with risk score levels. Using the prior example, your team might determine the following response-to-risk-score alignment:

Risk Score Level	Response
$150K and up	Address
$50K to $149K	Mitigate, Transfer, or Avoid
Under $49K	Watch

Based on the three example risks mentioned previously, the team would decide between:

- **Risk #1:** With a risk score of $100K, the team will determine between mitigating, transferring, or avoiding.

- **Risk #2:** With a risk score of $160K, the team will address the risk by immediately developing plans to add to the scope of the project.

- **Risk #3:** With a risk score of $9K, the team will watch the risk, monitoring for triggers to see if the risk actually occurs.

In my experience, the *avoid* and *transfer responses* are used less frequently than the *mitigate* and *accept responses*, but they are sometimes necessary. An example of the avoid response is when a sponsor chooses to not include a certain requirement or feature on a project because the team isn't sure the established timeframes or existing technologies will allow for it. The risk is typically a combination of poor quality, cost overruns, and/or missed dates, and the sponsor chooses to "defer" the requirement or feature until a later release, when more will be known. Since deferment removes the risk from the current scope, this is referred to as *risk avoidance.*

As an example of the transfer response from a software development project, we were uncertain of our team's ability to produce a feature as designed, and we reached out to another team that was utilizing the same platform and asked them to build the component we needed for our solution to work. In doing so, we transferred the risk of not delivering a piece of functionality to another project. While this meant we gave up the flexibility to change the underlying solution on our timetable, it did allow us to deliver our solution while hitting quality and feature expectations.

Risk Response: A Real-World Example

Earlier I mentioned that there are sometimes project stakeholders who treat all risks at DEFCON 1 levels, and I said that this is both unreasonable and a waste of time, energy, and money. Allow me to explain why I'm so adamant about this:

Several years ago, I joined a mobile device product team where the key stakeholders treated every risk like it was a meteor the size of Texas headed for the blue planet. In the mobile industry, competitive parity and speed to market are keys to survival, so frenetic energy and the loudest voices often rule the halls. When a new risk was identified, the stakeholders would demand immediate, "all hands on deck" attention to it. New meetings mushroomed up on people's calendars, and PowerPoint decks proliferated in response. It was, technically speaking, "crazy."

My solution to this Chicken Little mentality was to embrace transparency and create a simple risk log that included the following columns:

Column	Description
Risk Name	Allowed for creativity here as long as the name was unique.
Description	This had to include the effect any risk might cause. (Note: "the sky is falling" is not an effect; "we will die" is).
Trigger	Evidence to look for that indicates the risk has become realized.
Probability	The likelihood the risk would be realized.
Impact	The impact in dollars the risk would have on the project were it to materialize.
Score	Probability x Impact
Response	Address, Mitigate, Avoid, Transfer, or Watch.

As I added each new risk, I made sure that we identified and reviewed each of the columns, especially the Probability, Impact, and Score columns. We often had colorful debates about Probability, but Impact was often easy to agree upon. The next challenge would be deciding where we drew the line for our risk responses—specifically, which risks we would assign address and mitigate responses, and those we would assign the watch response. By assessing the risks in this way, we were making a distinction between those risks we must act upon and those we didn't have to do anything about. Simply having a clearly designated line meant we didn't have to react to all risks.

In addition to allowing for a prioritized and informed response to risks, this approach lowered the overall tension on the project, because it allowed us to focus on those risks that were of the highest priority.

We actually increased the total number of risks identified, because once we demonstrated a reasonable reaction to the assessed and prioritized risks, the ostriches among us were more willing to speak up. Not only did this boost my credibility with the stakeholders, it also allowed people to get on with their work.

PROACTIVE RISK MANAGEMENT: CONCLUSION

Risk assessment is where, as Ricky Bobby might say, the rubber meets the road. Without a way to assess and prioritize, all risks may appear equal. The risk assessment process, in contrast, enables the appropriate triaging and response for each risk—and it helps you gain buy-in from team members and stakeholders.

Of course, Risk Management is its own profession, and thus it would be insulting for me to attempt to cover the entire gamut of the discipline within a couple pages. However, the experiences I've had as a project manager have taught me how to proactively manage risks in order to increase the likelihood of my projects' success. When you include Proactive Risk Management in the art of Project Management, you are better prepared to set and manage the expectations of your sponsor and stakeholders, and better equipped to increase the value of their engagement in the project. When you use the risk assessment steps to help them prioritize risks; when you use the "Why won't this work?" process to present the truly significant risks to them; and when you demonstrate your leadership capabilities by focusing on the things that matter, you will engender sponsor and stakeholder trust and confidence in your ability to deliver on expectations.

KEY POINTS FOR CHAPTER 10:

- To produce results with great rewards, you must take on risks—and stakeholders' tolerance for risks are greatest at the beginning of the project.

- Every project will be knocked sideways by some unknown unknown—an unforeseeable event that will jeopardize the project's success. Therefore, the value of Proactive Risk Management is not to prevent the unforeseeable (since, by definition, this is impossible); instead, it is to create the process and cadence in dealing with issues and risks that will give your sponsor and stakeholders confidence in your ability to handle the big one, and will give you the bandwidth necessary to identify and focus when it does occur.

- "Why won't this work?" is a powerful risk identification technique in uncovering and resolving many of the reasons your team members may think they are on a fool's errand, and will likely identify a few crucial risks that will require your immediate attention and action.

- Developing a risk score for each identified risk by multiplying the risk impact by probability is a standard in the science of Project Management—you will determine which risks require attention and which do not.

CHAPTER 11

Checklist Item #8:

Taking Corrective Action

"No battle plan survives contact with the enemy."

—Colin Powell

Maybe you've heard the Project Management axiom "Plan the work, work the plan," which suggests there's value in both creating a plan and in closely managing that plan. But to Colin Powel's point, shouldn't you also have a plan for when the original plan doesn't work?

As mentioned before, the immutable law of Project Management is that somehow, somewhere, some unforeseen occurrence will knock your project sideways to the point of jeopardizing success and will force you, the project manager, to take serious corrective action to get back on track. Since this happens on all projects large and small, you would expect that the ability to "take corrective action" would be a core expectation of all projects managers, right? You'd expect it to be a key question in every project manager interview. You'd expect to see that specific capability listed on every project manager's job description. You'd expect to see classes teaching how to "take corrective action" at every professional education outlet. And of course you'd expect to see the capability highlighted in *A Guide to Project Management Body of Knowledge*[50]— the "Project Management bible," as some refer to it—right? Of course you would; unfortunately, you would be wrong.

According to the *Project Management Body of Knowledge*, affectionately referred to as the *PMBOK*, the definition of corrective action is *"An intentional activity that realigns the performance of the project work with the project management plan."*[51] Allow me to paraphrase: *When stuff goes wrong, you'll need a plan and activities to get you back on track.* Pretty underwhelming, right?

I find this definition to be lacking because in my experience, every project will experience at least one unforeseen problem that significantly threatens the successful outcome of the project. I cannot say with 100% accuracy that all projects will experience a significant problem, but I am totally comfortable saying that 99.9% of projects will.

Taking corrective action is the most important thing a project manager can do to guide their project to a successful conclusion. Since every project has at least one unforeseen problem arise that threatens the successful outcome of the project, every successful project manager, then, would benefit from having a plan for when "the plan" doesn't work. In case you don't have a plan for when the big one hits, here are the steps you can execute to take correction action and get back on track.

"A problem is a chance for you to do your best."
　　　　　　　　　　　　　　　　　　—Duke Ellington

---

50. The *PMBOK* is developed and published by the Project Management Institute. For more information, go to www.pmi.org.

51. *A Guide to Project Management Body of Knowledge Version 5*, Project Management Institute, pg. 81

STEP 1: SOLVE THE SIMPLE STUFF— EMBRACING THE VALUE OF RISK MANAGEMENT

As you just read in the last chapter, Proactive Risk Management is the practice of identifying all known risks, assessing and prioritizing each one, and then repeating this process regularly in order to maintain an awareness of risks throughout the project. The real value of Risk Management is eliminating and/or creating a plan for all the significant known unknowns. This allows you to:

1. Manage and prevent any known issue from becoming something that might threaten your achievement of project objectives.

2. Earn the confidence from stakeholders that they can take any necessary corrective action.

3. Create the bandwidth for dealing with whatever unknown has just rocked your project team's world.

Having the bandwidth to deal with the "big one" is critical, since the significant issues that knock the project sideways sometimes go undetected for some time—which only exacerbates its impact. Performing Risk Management also has a positive impact on key stakeholder engagement, because it increases stakeholders' level of trust and confidence in your abilities to lead the project. When you demonstrate your ability to manage risk, your stakeholders will be more likely to allow you to lead when something happens to send your project sideways—and more likely to follow you. To increase your project's likelihood of success, you need to have all stakeholders participating in positive ways and not questioning your abilities to lead the team out of the forest. This is crucial.

STEP 2: SOLVE THE DIFFICULT STUFF— A REPEATABLE PROBLEM-SOLVING FRAMEWORK

"We've never lost an American in space and we're sure as hell not gonna lose one on my watch! Failure is not an option."

—Gene Krantz, Flight Director, Apollo 13

To help you deal with your project when it go sideways, you should have a repeatable problem-solving framework plan that will allow you to react positively to the unforeseeable when it does occur. When Jim Lovell said "Houston, we have a problem," and when Captain Sullenburger called out "Bird strike," both captains were staring significant, life-threatening problems in the face. A problem is a problem no matter its level of significance, and a proven, repeatable approach for problem-solving is a leader's—and a successful project manager's—best friend.

Years ago, I was in search of a proven, repeatable problem-solving framework, and my search led me to the universal source of knowledge: Wikipedia. When I searched on problem-solving processes, I was thankfully introduced to Alex Osborn[52] and Dr. Sydney Parnes, and my problem-solving days have been better ever since.

Mr. Osborn and Dr. Parnes developed the Creative Problem Solving Process[53] in the 1950s. Their process recommends:

1. Gathering data and performing root-cause analysis before jumping to conclusions.
2. Obtaining stakeholder alignment on the problem statement, ensuring the solution will target the "right" problem as far as all stakeholders are concerned.

---

52. Alex Osborn is also known as the godfather of brainstorming. For more information, go to http://en.wikipedia.org/wiki/Brainstorming

53. For more information on the Creative Problem Solving Process, please check out the Creative Education Foundation at http://www.creativeeducationfoundation.org

3. Creating solutions that are focused on root causes, not just symptoms.

The Creative Problem Solving Process is fairly simple, yet I've used it to help solve various unforeseen problems on my projects (as well as the problem of where to take my wife for dinner). Large and small problems—it works for both. Here are the six steps:

1. **Objective Finding**—What is the goal that will be attained by solving the problem?

2. **Fact Finding**—What is the evidence of this problem?

3. **Problem Solving**—What is the problem statement, and does everyone agree that this is the problem?

4. **Idea Finding**—What are some of the possible solutions to this problem?

5. **Solution Finding**—Based on the identified goals, what solution best resolves the problem?

6. **Acceptance Finding**—What are the steps to implement the solution and confirm that it has solved the problem?

Utilizing this repeatable framework for all problems can help you build stakeholder confidence in your ability to handle things when they go wrong, and it will also help you train your team to successfully take on problems.

The framework also helps in tackling bigger issues: Several years back and after being on a client engagement for two weeks, my client, whose team was having trouble meeting expectations, asked me what I thought the problem was. I told him that after being on-site for only two weeks, I had heard a lot of opinions but hadn't fully formed my own yet. The client then proceeded to share his opinion of what the problem was: "project management."

A couple of months passed, my familiarity with the client's team grew, and as we launched the project, I reflected back on the conversation we'd had and decided to perform the first three steps of the Creative Problem Solving Process by myself. The goal was simple enough: increase collaboration and productivity amongst the team. For evidence gathering, I interviewed several team members, performing the "Five Whys" technique for identifying root causes (I'll describe that technique in detail in Chapter 15). Based on the information I gathered, I created a problem statement and then asked the client out for coffee to share the process and data I had gathered.

One of the additional benefits of following the six-step Creative Problem Solving Process is that when presenting the information back to a client or stakeholders, it's easy for them to follow the bouncing ball as you walk them through the process. This is exactly what occurred during my conversation with the client, and it resulted in a great conversation about what we could do next to engage his management team in steps four through six and create the solutions we were looking for. And over the next three months, we did just that.

STEP 3: DON'T FREAK OUT—FOCUSING ON THE RIGHT THING AT THE RIGHT TIME

"Never let them see you sweat" is an idea made famous years ago by a deodorant commercial, but I think the concept is better portrayed in the following story:

There was once a treasure ship on its way back to port. About halfway there, it was approached by a pirate ship, its skull-

and-crossbones flag waving in the breeze! "Captain, Captain, what shall we do?" asked the first mate.

"Go to my cabin and bring me my red shirt," said the captain. The first mate did so. And wearing his bright red shirt, the captain exhorted his crew to fight. So inspiring was he, that the pirate ship was repelled without casualties.

A few days later, the ship was again approached, this time by two pirate ships.

"Captain, Captain, what should we do?" the first mate cried.

The Captain replied, "Bring me my red shirt!"

The crew, emboldened by their fearless captain, fought heroically and managed to defeat both boarding parties, though they took many casualties. That night, the survivors had a great celebration. The first mate asked the captain the secret of his bright red shirt.

"It's quite simple," the captain said. "If I am wounded, the blood does not show, and the crew continues to fight without fear."

A week passed, and they were nearing their home port when suddenly the lookout cried that ten ships from the enemy's armada were approaching!

"Captain, captain, we're in terrible trouble, what do we do?" the first mate cried, looking expectantly at the miracle worker.

Pale with fear, the captain commanded, "First mate, bring me my brown pants!"

As I said in Chapter 8, if everyone on the project is freaking out, the project manager should be calm and elevate everyone to the big picture—but if everyone is calm, the project manager should be worried about all the things that could go wrong." Allow me to elaborate

on that concept. When everyone is freaking out (which will likely occur when the project is knocked sideways), that's not the time for you
to be *visibly* freaking out as well. Internally, sure, go right ahead—but
externally, you need to be a rock for your team members. In accordance
with the teachings of the field of Emotional Intelligence, don't discount
the team's "freak out"; be empathetic and assure your team members
that you understand why they are worried. But don't forget that as the
project manager, you are expected to lead your team out of *Freak-Out
City*, and the way to do that is to:

1. Go big-picture with the team by providing the project vision you advocated for (as highlighted in the first principle
   of professional project leadership—see Chapter 8)

2. Clearly tie the problem-solving effort to the project's decision-making criteria as set forth by the project's objectives
   (see our discussion about setting clear business objectives
   in Chapter 6)

3. Using a repeatable problem-solving framework

Freaking out is the natural reaction to not knowing how to resolve
a problem, and from time to time, your team, stakeholders, and sponsor
maybe fall prey to this behavior. As the project manager, however, even
if you don't know the best solution to the problem at hand, you at least
know how to *approach* any problem—so it stands to reason that there is
no reason or value in you freaking out.

TAKING CORRECTIVE ACTION: CONCLUSION

"Everyone has a plan, until they get punched in the mouth."

—Mike Tyson

A project manager's ability to take corrective action is critical to their being able to deliver successful project outcomes, and it is amazing to me that this skill is not one of the core elements of every Project Management curriculum or certification program. Perhaps we should change the Project Management saying from "Plan the work, work the plan" to something even better: "Plan the work, work the plan, then have a plan to re-plan when the plan doesn't work." As both Colin Powell and Mike Tyson, two very different warriors, have highlighted, the original plan is perfect—until you have to start following it. So, with this in mind, having a plan for when the original plan doesn't work is another cornerstone to project success.

To successfully lead projects, you must have the skills and abilities to tackle significant project problems, and this requires having a plan for leading your team through the unknown. The Creative Problem Solving Process provides you with a great, repeatable framework for leading teams when the project gets "punched in the mouth"—and sends it back in the right direction, towards the successful delivery of project objectives.

KEY POINTS FOR CHAPTER 11:

- The skills and ability to take corrective action is required on all projects because every original plan will prove to be deficient at some point in a project. Having a talent for taking corrective action is so important to project success that it should not only be part of all Project Management training, certifications, and job requirements, it should also be a major contributing factor to how a project manager is evaluated and compensated.

- Proactive Risk Management helps a project manager prepare for the opportunity to perform taking corrective action, but it does not prevent the need for it.

- The Creative Problem Solving Process is a great framework for all problem-solving, but especially for taking corrective action, because when the stakes are high (the project's success is in jeopardy), the quality of the solution needs to be high, and stakeholders need to be in alignment on the problem, the right solution, and the measurement of validation.

- No project has ever benefitted from a project manager freaking out in a moment of crisis. Don't be that project manager. Trust the process, follow the right steps, be a leader.

CHAPTER 12

Checklist Item #9:

Fostering Joint Accountability

Imagine this: An organization that celebrates its successes, both large and small, and also embraces its failures, so that it rewards the wins and reinforces a culture of learning and improvement. In this organization, individuals identify others' contributions to success and also freely stand up to take personal responsibility when things go wrong. Sounds like a utopian workplace that only exists in management philosophy books, right?

Well, maybe it is Pollyanna-ish to presume that a culture of accountability is possible within a large organization. Maybe it is unlikely that leaders who rely on punishment as their form of accountability, or lack the knowledge of what accountability truly means, can repeatedly demonstrate strong and healthy accountability behavior. Accountability, however, is a key behavior you want your team members and stakeholders to embrace and exhibit.

If you are fortunate enough to be able to select team members and stakeholders who already act with accountability, you are living the good life. But the rest of us need to be proactive in fostering joint accountability amongst the team, as this is how the best teams coalesce, compete, and succeed together.

In order to lead successful projects, you will want to establish and cultivate a team culture of joint accountability—which, in turn, will result in a culture of winning.

THE BEATINGS WILL CONTINUE UNTIL MORALE IMPROVES

I used to be skeptical that joint accountability was something that teams could exhibit. In my experience, it was the rare individual who took responsibility when mistakes were made. Remember the matrix-organized company I used to work for that I talked about in Chapter 8? At that company, there was an expectation that matrix relationships would enable innovation, collaboration, and success because of the sense of "shared accountability." When things went well, there was definitely a sense of "shared success" or "shared contribution" to the success. However, when things went wrong, that "shared accountability" crumbled into "no accountability"; I witnessed a lot of finger-pointing, a lot of flaming e-mails written in ALL CAPs, and a lot of complaining in the hallway about those in influential and decision-making positions—none of it productive.

Prior to my time at that company, I worked in an organization that *did* hold people "accountable"—however, the form of accountability the leaders embraced there could only be described as punishment. People did what they were told out of fear of punishment. Of course, that meant when something went wrong, everyone simply said, "I just did what I was told." People were truly afraid of doing something different (e.g., innovate, improve, etc.) because fear of the punishment was greater than any possible reward.

Neither of these companies had a *true* culture of accountability, and accordingly, employees and leaders demonstrated behavior that reflected that gap. As a project manager in those companies, when things went wrong, it was always challenging and time-consuming to get team members to go beyond blamestorming and on to something productive, like resolving the issues. I wasn't naïve enough to think that I could change the organizations' cultures, but I did want to know how I might be able to influence the behavior of my team members.

THERE'S GOT TO BE ANOTHER WAY

While reading *The Oz Principle* by Roger Connors, Tom Smith, and Craig Hickman a few years later, I learned a new process for producing a culture of "joint accountability" that challenged my previous experience and gave me hope that I had found a way to proactively influence the behavior of my team. The authors prescribe a three-step process for establishing joint accountability on teams:

1. Set clear role and responsibility expectations with team members

2. Have team members individually ask two questions when something goes wrong

3. Establish the behavior of reminding others when they act without accountability

I like three-step processes, but I was skeptical of whether these steps would work for me. Fortunately, I was able to immediately put it to the test on my project. Here is what I did:

1) Set Clear Expectations

Fostering joint accountability requires establishing what it means to act with accountability on your team. And as *The Oz Principle* authors astutely note, it's not fair to hold someone accountable without setting clear expectations for their roles and responsibilities.

Most project managers attempt to do this by managing project schedules and developing RACI charts. But successful project managers will go further, and identify behavioral and stakeholder expectations. The three suggestions Connors, Smith, and Hickman offer regarding expectation-setting with team members are to:

1. Make the expectations clear and attainable

2. Establish the limit of the expectation

3. Identify support for fulfilling the expectation

Once you have identified those role and responsibility expectations, your team will be ready to have a dialogue about what it means to behave with accountability.

2) Acting with Accountability

Once clear expectations have been set, the successful project manager will define what it means to act with accountability, as well as identify the behaviors that demonstrate what *not* acting with accountability looks like.

We're familiar with the behaviors that show a lack of accountability:

- Blaming others

- Pointing fingers

- Telling stories

- Asking what you should do

The authors refer to those behaviors as being "beyond the line," as in, the "line of accountability." In order to act above the line—to act *with* accountability—the authors suggest that each individual ask two questions when a problem occurs:

1. What did I do to help contribute to the problem?

2. What can we do to move toward desired results?

That's it. It's beautiful in its simplicity. Those two questions alone will drive individuals to act with accountability. Answering those questions honestly will lead you to quickly identify options for resolving the issues. The first question requires humility on the part of the individual—and by publically asking and answering this question, others are more likely to reciprocate and also contribute to identifying where the issues were created. The answers to the second question will drive collaborative solutions and allow for "yes, and" thinking, where the team builds on ideas for resolving the issues.

Going through the exercise of answering both questions in the absence of those non-accountable behaviors (e.g., finger-pointing, CYA, etc.), your team will foster a more open, collaborative, and honest environment. This is necessary for the third step to take effect and cultivate true joint accountability.

3) Holding Each Other Accountable

Achieving joint accountability, or being successful at holding others accountable, is really quite simple once expectations are established and the team individually exhibits the behaviors of asking the two accountability questions. When those things are in place, the only thing team members need to do is gently remind other members when they are doing anything other than asking the two accountability questions in step two.

Remember that individual accountability is simply asking yourself two questions when any problem occurs:

1. How did I contribute to the problem?

2. What can we do to move toward desired results?

With that as the definition, any time that someone is engaged in pointing fingers, complaining, or playing the self-preservation game of CYA, they are not acting with personal accountability. And if the project manager has already set the expectation for "joint accountability," team members will be able to remind that person about the two accountability questions.

Holding each other accountable is not telling other people how they've contributed to the problem, nor is it telling them how they can help move your team toward results—it is simply letting your teammates know if and when they falter. If "joint accountability" has been set up correctly, the likely response should be, "Oh, you are right, thank you. Let me get on that" (At least, that is what should be said out loud!).

WINNING

Not long after reading *The Oz Principle*, I worked with a client whose team was having a hard time demonstrating accountability. The issue was exacerbated by stakeholders who leaned toward the "beating" side of accountability, such as publicly humiliating people for their mistakes. Just like other things that gravitate downhill, the client wasn't immune to partaking in this shared manifestation of "holding people accountable" when something went wrong, either.

I counseled the client that while the prevailing brand of accountability—punishment—was something that wasn't going to be remedied overnight, he *could* change the definition of accountability on his team.

He agreed to try, and we took the team on *The Oz Principle* journey, first by having the whole team read the book and discuss the principles, then by putting them into effect. They liked this approach, and thought it was especially funny when someone used a mocking tone when saying, "My contribution to this problem was _____, and this is how I think WE can move it forward toward desired results . . ." Someone else would reply in an equally mocking voice, "Yes, well my contribution was _____, and I think we should do _____ to solve the issue." And on they went—but mock as they might, they were putting the *Oz Principle's* individual accountability behavior into practice.

Now, of course it wasn't easy to change the behavior of the team, and we did have to start from the top down with leadership. Successful organizational behavioral change requires change from both the team *and* the leader, and it usually requires more change on the part of the leader. New habits are hard to form; therefore, the leader needs to reinforce the desired behavior. The first time someone acted below the line (that is, acted without taking accountability) for example, instead of reminding the person to act with accountability like we had agreed, my client sent the person the PowerPoint slide from our *Oz Principle* book club presentation that outlined the "below the line" and "above the line" accountability behaviors. Similar to a soccer referee handing out a yellow card to a rule-breaking player, the client chose a nonverbal and private way to remind the person of the team expectations.

Unfortunately, that is not the ideal way to reinforce the right behavior. When I heard about the "yellow carding" incident, I reminded the client that there are many ways to prompt people to act with accountability, but that "yellow carding" them feels more like a punishment. It would have been far more valuable for the individual, and the team, to have spoken up in the meeting and demonstrated to everyone how to remind someone of the desired accountability steps. This public reinforcing, when done respectfully, can be a positive and impactful form of driving accountability.

PSEUDO ACCOUNTABILITY?

After reading one of my blogs about fostering joint accountability, one reader submitted a comment that in essence said that fostering joint accountability is "pseudo accountability"—that it says, "you have to be accountable, but don't you dare hold anyone else accountable." The reader was basically suggesting that fostering joint accountability isn't feasible because it lacks the teeth of the traditional performance management techniques, which tell you to hold people's feet to the fire when things don't get done.

I was grateful for the reader's comment, because it gave me the opportunity to respond. Fostering joint accountability should be thought of as an "and" approach, not an "or" approach. It's not about replacing longstanding practices and setting role expectations through performance measurement. Those things are crucial to setting the right expectations with employees and ensuring that they are focused on the drivers to the organizational objectives; they're also the tools we need to manage our poor performers when they fail to deliver desired results. They are like guardrails on the freeway: it's great to have them to prevent a catastrophic event, like going over a cliff or into oncoming traffic, but when you plow up against them, you still suffer significant damage.

There is a time and place to hold individuals accountable when their performance is below target—but fostering joint accountability is about setting expectations for the desired, positive behaviors when something goes wrong so individuals start engaging in correcting mistakes *before* they are told or forced to. Which environment will most people want to work in: a) one where you and your coworkers attempt to hide mistakes and are punished or publically shamed when those mistakes are discovered, or b) one where mistakes are tolerated and people work together to resolve issues quickly and move on? Most of us will pick option b— but most of us don't have individual performance metrics that create that type of environment.

Since most of us are not measured by our contribution to solving problems and most project managers do not have authority over the individuals on their project, we must rely on our ability to influence team members to "do the right thing" when we're managing a project, *most especially* when something goes wrong. Fostering joint accountability is a proactive approach to creating a team-shared value about tolerating mistakes, and working individually and collaboratively to fix those mistakes to move on toward the desired objectives.

FOSTERING JOINT ACCOUNTABILITY: CONCLUSION

Fostering joint accountability means *informing others when they are not acting with accountability.* Instead of chastising someone when they haven't done what they agreed to do—which will likely lead to a defensive response involving excuses for why the task wasn't performed—you simply remind them by helping the individual re-focus on those two important questions, "*How did I contribute?*" and "*What can we do to move forward?*" In doing so, the leader will help to cultivate a culture of joint accountability and ultimately help the team be more proactive and constructive.

In my experience, the successful completion of most tasks and deliverables are dependent upon a series of inputs from others, and embracing the concept of fostering joint accountability reflects that reality. Between inputs and outputs, handoffs, multi-threaded communications, and integrated project planning, we are too interdependent in project environments for any one individual to truly be an owner and fully, *independently* accountable.

It is likely that you will run into issues so frequently on your projects that you will have the opportunity to demonstrate your own personal accountability by publicly asking those two questions aloud. To foster joint accountability amongst your teams, you should collectively agree on the definition and expectation for "accountability," then agree on how to remind others when they do not act within our agreed standards. When individuals on a team hold each other jointly accountable in a positive way, behavioral changes occur that strengthen the team dynamic and increase productivity, rather than tear the team down.

KEY POINTS FOR CHAPTER 12:

* In order to hold your team members, stakeholders, and sponsors accountable, you must first establish clear expectations for each individual. You must also ensure that you understand their expectations of you when it comes to holding them accountable.

* As the project manager, you demonstrate accountability by not blaming others when problems occur, and instead by modeling the two questions highlighted by the authors of *The Oz Principle*: 1) How did I contribute to this problem? and 2) What can we do to move toward desired results? Modeling this behavior will focus the team on fixing the problem and achieving desired results rather than engaging in non-accountable behavior, such as finger-pointing, CYA, and blamestorming.

* Holding each other accountable, per *The Oz Principle*, means reminding others when they are not focused on answering those two questions, or when they are actively demonstrating non-accountable behavior.

* Fostering joint accountability does not replace traditional performance management practices or holding people accountable for poor performance (i.e., firing them). As a

project manager, however, rarely do you have direct line of reporting responsibilities for your teammates, and it is much more advantageous to incentivize the right behaviors than it is to punish bad ones.

CHAPTER 13

Checklist Item #10:

Skilled Resources

Project success is dependent upon having the right resources doing the right work at the right time. That might seem like the great understatement of this book, but it's not exactly as straightforward as it seems. Presuming that you have shepherded the process to a place where appropriate scope has been identified and the critical path and schedule dependencies have been aligned with the business objectives and vision of the project, let's talk about getting the right people assigned and performing the work.

The right resources will have three characteristics: capability, experience, and motivation. In other words, they can do the work, they've done similar work before, and they're inspired to succeed.

CAPABILITY

When identifying scope and associated tasks and deliverables, you should also ensure that appropriate resource capability requirements are identified; that way, you will be able to articulate the request for the right resources. Doing this early in the process will help ensure that the project doesn't have people lacking the skills required to do the job, and it should also prevent over-clubbing—or rather, assigning a resource with a skill level well above what is required.

It's pretty easy to understand why you would not want under-skilled people on your project; why, though, would over-skilled people be something to avoid just as much? One of the best examples I can think of relates it to golfing: you wouldn't bring out your driver to tee off on a 95-yard hole (unless you want to pay for someone's window a block behind the green). Over-clubbing with regards to resources can have as disastrous effects as under-clubbing. While junior resources in senior roles can create defects and rework when their efforts fail to meet expectations, senior resources in junior roles can also create rework when they over-engineer solutions that do not fit into the rest of the solution.

As an example, I once took over a project from a project manager who, in an attempt to please the business sponsor, had tried to collect a level of detail on the project at a finer grain than what was normally collected by project managers in the organization. This created an unrealistic expectation with the business sponsor, and ultimately failed when team members rejected the idea of tracking their time at the task level when the project management system only required time tracking at the project level. Additionally, since team members were employees and projects were only billed for forty hours maximum, regardless of how many hours were submitted, as long as tasks were completed on schedule, there was no impact to schedule or budget. In fact, because of all the overtime employees spent, the project budget was spared a 10% surcharge (if the hours had actually been charged), so when the project manager reported the hour overages, he painted a false picture of the budgetary impacts of the work taking more hours than had been estimated.

A similar example is the time I worked with another project manager who knew MS Project backward and forward. I'm pretty sure she was able to guide satellites and program her TIVO based on her power user knowledge of MS Project. She would literally spend three hours a day using it, and could report on incredible details about her project (e.g., Monte Carlo-like scenario planning with her Critical Path, and average labor rates for Tuesdays), except for one important detail: how it was going. She spent so much time gathering and crunching data in MS Project, she sacrificed time spent talking to team members. When the team announced a two-week slip flipping the project into red, the project manager was as surprised as the sponsors were.

In order to have the right resources on your project, in addition to the right capabilities, you should be looking for the right level of experience and motivation. Let's talk about examples of both.

EXPERIENCE

"I have not failed 1,000 times. I have successfully discovered 1,000 ways to NOT make a light bulb."

—Thomas Edison

Several years ago in my hometown of Seattle, voters approved three successive initiatives to create the Seattle Monorail Project, a public transportation system in the image of the monorail from the 1962 Seattle World's Fair, which would stretch fourteen miles from the northwest end of town, through downtown, and out to West Seattle. After getting the affirming votes, the county started buying up property and raising taxes in anticipation of building the line. Then the finance manager for the project published the details for how the project would be financed: $4 billion in project costs that would ultimately cost the county $11 billion due to interest payments over forty years.[54] As quick as you can say, "Take the bus," another initiative was on the ballot and the unsustainable monorail dream was crushed.

---

54. "No painless solution to monorail crisis," by Drew DeSilver in *The Seattle Times*, July 5, 2005

Now, $7 billion in interest payments for a $4 billion project sounds outrageous. Funny thing is, it's pretty standard. The Kingdome, Seattle's indoor stadium which opened in 1977, cost $67 million to build, $40 million of which was publicly funded, and when it was demolished to create Seahawk Stadium (currently called CenturyLink Field), we still owed $127 million in public financing for the Kingdome[55]—talk about being leveraged!

So why did the Monorail project go sideways? The *Seattle Times* reported that the finance manager had never worked on a mega construction project before, and therefore did not know the nuances of how to handle these types of situations and how to message the project financial plan. Inexperience killed the Monorail.[56]

Now, I love the challenge of attempting something new, but I will only do it when working with some safety net, usually under the guidance of a strong mentor or coach.

A prerequisite for a meaningful experience is that the individual pay attention to the lessons learned from the experience. I'm sure we know project managers who tout ten to twenty years of experience, but if the type of projects they are managing are not that different from the ones they started on at the beginning of their career, perhaps one could say that they have one year of experience, ten to twenty times over. Experience should be the collection of successes plus the summary of lessons learned from failures. I have much more faith in someone who can apply the lessons learned from mistakes versus someone who has not yet failed. Of course, it's always a lot easier if we can learn from other people's mistakes, which is why I wrote this book—so you can learn from mine.

---

55. "Taxpayers Should Sacrifice Kingdome To Save Seahawks," by Blaine Newnham in *The Seattle Times*, March 23, 1997

56. "Monorail finance plan abandoned," by Mike Lindblom in *The Seattle Times*, July 1, 2005

MOTIVATION

Motivation, like communication, is a two-way street—sender and receiver must both be turned on. Sure, leaders should provide a vision for a project and attempt to align the interests of individuals with the interests of an organization. This is a good recipe for motivating great work. However, the recipient of that motivation holds the cards in this game; if they are not willing or choose not to be motivated, then game over. They need to come to the table ready to play.

Research that the Gallup organization conducted on the willingness of employees to participate in organizational change found that 17% of employees, nearly one in five, will actively disengage in these change initiatives.[57] While that's a lot of people like Wally from Dilbert, that means 83% of employees are open to change and can be motivated to buy into a new direction. Remember when I mentioned author Daniel Pink's assertion in *Drive: The Surprising Truth About What Motivates Us*[58]—that employees need three things to be motivated, and those three things are not cash, money, and compensation? While conventional wisdom, as captured by Jack Welch, says "you get the behaviors you *reward* and measure," Mr. Pink cites research showing that when tasks require more cogitation than simple routines, cash rewards actually reduced performance. Once people are satisfied with compensation, he says, the three things that motivate employees are autonomy, mastery, and purpose.

You would think that *autonomy* is easy to achieve these days, as people complain about having to do the job of two or three people (managers are too busy to micromanage, right?), but this type of autonomy refers to being empowered to make decisions about how they do their work. *Mastery* means allowing employees to have the opportunity to obtain skills and grow talents that can be applied to their work. Lastly, *purpose* is a synonym for vision—employees need to buy into

---

57. *Terms of Engagement*, Dick Axelrod, 2001
58. *Drive: The Surprising Truth About What Motivates Us*, **Daniel Pink, 2009**

the purpose of a project in order form them to be motivated. In other words, "Tell me why we are doing it, and allow me to determine what we do and how we do it, and make sure I have the knowledge to do it right, and then I'll be all in." Does this sound like something a motivated employee might say? Does it sound like something you might say?

Well, it sounds like something I might say, and as the Information Age has inverted the organizational pyramid as far as where information resides and how work gets done within an company, I think focusing on autonomy, mastery, and purpose is an approach that makes a lot of sense. We still need leaders to point people in a direction by providing a vision, but then we should be able to rely on people to determine how to achieve that direction, and not get in the way and tell them how to do their work.

SKILLED RESOURCES: CONCLUSION

I always feel a little embarrassed when I come to the "Skilled Resources" factor on my *Project Success Checklist* presentation. It's the most "brush your teeth and comb your hair" of all the success factors, and usually at least one person will say aloud, "Well, duh." (Okay, sometimes that person is me). However, top talent is not always available on projects, and the successful project manager will need to understand how to resource their team, as well as what to look for, and look out for, when reviewing resource assignments. The right type of capable, the right kind of experience, and the ability to be motivated are keys to having the right resources on teams. And just like Soylent Green,[59] project success is made of people.

---

59. *Soylent Green* is a 1973 dystopian science-fiction movie in which Charleton Heston famously discovers (and then passionately announces) that Soylent Green, an elixir for overpopulation and depleted resources, is actually made from people. The movie is cited as causing another generation of American youth to despise and detest their vegetables (okay, I made that last part up).

KEY POINTS FOR CHAPTER 13:

- Having the right resources on the project team is the most intuitive success factor on my Project Success Checklist: you need the right people to do the right work and produce the right results. Duh (there, I said it so hopefully you don't have to).

- The three key ingredients for having the right resources on your project is a balance of capability, experience, and motivation.

- Over-skilled resources can be as detrimental to your project as having under-skilled resources, because they tend to over-engineer solutions and create more work than is necessary to achieve desired objectives (believe me, I know; I've been that over-skilled resource who created more work than is necessary).

- Being capable of performing work is not the same as having the experience to do that work, just like following a recipe does not make you a master chef. You need to be careful about one's claim to experience; just because they've been in the industry for some time, it doesn't mean that they've been paying attention and learning from their mistakes.

- Motivation is the accelerator in performance—a team must have a passion to get the job done and done correctly in order to be considered "high-performing." This requires both manager and employee to embrace the vision and deliver on passion. If the relation goes in only one direction, you cannot be successful.

CHAPTER 14

Checklist Item #11:

Organizational Change Management

"There is nothing more difficult to take in hand, more perilous to conduct, or more uncertain in its success, than to take the lead in the introduction of a new order of things."

—Machiavelli

Which is more critical to project success: Organizational Change Management or Project Management?

Before you answer, let me tell you about two examples that might impact your response. Like many project managers, I've been on a few projects where I was able to appropriately set and deliver on expectations on scope, schedule, and budget ("on time, on budget, high five!")—only to have the end product of the project be declared a big fat zero in the marketplace.

One project I successfully led to an on-schedule and on-budget release had to be turned off six hours after being launched. The features in the newly released product generated such negative reaction in the marketplace that our company experienced a huge spike in complaints to the call center. The call volume was so high, in fact, that it triggered a rarely used company policy allowing our customer care team to remove a new release from production without even conferring with our product owner first. Ouch.

If the measurement of success in these cases was whether the project delivered on scope, schedule, and budget—i.e., the holy trinity of Project Management—we nailed it. However, if the success was measured by ROI—which it should be, by the way—it was an undeniable failure. With this project and any other project where I have successfully delivered the project on time and on budget yet the end product landed flat, we obviously had not done enough work to a) confirm that customers wanted the product or b) prepare users for the product.

Contrast that experience with the time when I took over Project Management duties several months after the previous project manager was "forced" into agreeing to unreasonable expectations for scope, schedule, and budget. By "forced," I mean he was unsuccessful in his negotiations with the business owner, who had unreasonable demands for said project scope, schedule, and budget. To make matters worse, the project manager lacked sponsorship from his management, so he had no backup in his attempts to appropriately set expectations.

Sure enough, by the time I had arrived, the budget had been blown out of the water and the target launch date was in serious jeopardy. The project was in such a bad place that the corrective action plan I came up with showed that we'd only be able to hit our schedule if we increased our team size, which meant a 50% increase in budget and lowering our priority requirements into a future phase of development.

Luckily, even with all of these challenges and performance issues, the project team had done one thing extremely well—they had gotten customers involved in the project from day one. They had ensured that users were involved in identifying why the new product was needed by engaging them to review prototypes, help test features, and even train other users in how to use the new product. Because of this, once we launched—even though we needed 50% more money and had to defer some features that were originally promised—the products landed extremely well with the target audience. And since the users were successfully able to use the product to do their jobs, the product delivered on its expected benefits to the organization, maximizing its ROI even with the budget issues. Senior leadership and users, forgetting all of the scope, schedule, and budget challenges, declared the project a big success. Of course, if you asked the people who were on the project team what their level of satisfaction with the project was, they'd say somewhere in between "low" and "couldn't get any lower." They'd had a vitriolic relationship with the business owner, and had put in months of overtime. Not one of them would declare the project a success—nor would they want to duplicate the experience.

Let's look at the scoreboard: In the first project, we nailed Project Management nirvana by delivering on scope, schedule, and budget; however, because we ignored Organizational Change Management, it was a failure. In the second project, we failed on Project Management, but we nailed Organizational Change Management, and the project was deemed a huge success. Now, back to the original question: Which is more critical to project success, Project Management or Organizational Change Management?

I will borrow a principle from improvisational comedy and answer with a, "Yes, and . . ." Imagine if we nailed both disciplines of Project Management and Organizational Change Management on a project. *That* would be a recipe for success.

HOW ORGANIZATIONAL CHANGE MANAGEMENT IMPACTS PROJECT SUCCESS

Every project attempts to introduce a change for a target audience. Projects are approved and funded with the expectation of achieving an economic result, and that result requires a change, on some level, in behaviors and actions. Whether the project is implementing a new payroll system or producing a new aircraft, the project will introduce a change.

The discipline of Organizational Change Management (OCM) is a systematic approach for cultivating leadership support and end user acceptance for the attainment of a successful change. OCM can target organizational behavior and performance; for instance, it can be used to attempt to increase the amount of accountable behavior exhibited by management. OCM can also be applied to attain adoption of the end product of a project. In both instances, the framework and approach can be similar, just as Project Management is similar on small- and large-scale projects. That's not the only similarity between the two disciplines.

The Standish Group's Chaos research, however controversial, shows that roughly 30% of IT projects are delivered on time and on budget. Not great results. The research on change initiative success rates, such as IBM's Making Change Work[60] and McKinsey Consulting's Change Management[61] research and others, points to an eerily similar 30% success rate. I think those success rates *are* an indication of practitioner performance in both disciplines, but *not* an indication of our capabilities to execute the work—I believe it comes down to how we identify and address stakeholder expectations. Specifically, if we do not discover expectations and/or as soon as we allow unrealistic stakeholder expectations to go unaddressed, we're heading off the rails. Of course, there are poor-performing practitioners out there, but I believe the key word in the statement "70% of initiatives achieve less than expected results" is "expected."

---

60. IBM's Making Change Work can be found here: http://www.ibm.com/gbs/makingchangework
61. McKinsey's Organizing for Successful Change Management Global Survey can be found here: http://www.mckinseyquarterly.com/Organization/Change_Management/Organizing_for_successful_change_management_A_McKinsey_Global_Survey_1809

DO WE REALLY NEED TO DO BOTH?

When I share with project managers that OCM increases the likelihood of a project's success, I usually get an exasperated look that seems to say, "*What?!?! I'm too busy doing Project Management, I can't also do Change Management!*" My response is always the same: "You should focus your limited time and energy on what contributes most to success." If that means you are faced with the decision to either engage with an influential member of the targeted user community who is experiencing problems with your project or complete your status report, I recommend you do the former.

More recently I've been adding a question which I learned from Tim Creasey, Prosci's Chief Development Officer: "How many of the project's benefits require user adoption?" In a lot of cases, many if not all of the project benefits require user adoption in some form. In that case, since a successful project requires adoption of the end product, OCM is a critical success factor for projects, and therefore project managers need to ensure OCM is within the scope of the project.

Prosci, an industry leader in Change Management research, recently reported that organizations that apply a formal Change Management methodology are six times more likely to achieve project objectives and meet stakeholders' expectations than those organizations that don't.[62] As I've said before, achieving project success is a difficult endeavor; if I know my odds increase six-fold when I incorporate OCM principles, I would be foolish not to do so—and so would you.

3 PRINCIPLES OF OCM

So, how does the successful project manager adopt OCM without having to do two jobs, or attempting to do too much? Some initiatives will benefit from a dedicated OCM approach that will be separate from the Project Management focus. That said, there will be plenty of projects where OCM will not be a separate function, and in those instances, the

---

62. "Best Practices in Change Management Report" 2014 Edition, Prosci Benchmarking Report, page 14

project manager can absolutely adopt key OCM principles to successfully drive adoption of the end product. Here are three principles that I
recommend all project managers perform to drive adoption:

1) Change Impact Analysis

Change Impact Analysis identifies—in detail—the changes that impact
each role by determining:

- the processes that are changing

- the roles impacted by the process changes

- the behaviors and actions that employees are expected to do
  differently in the future

Once you've done this, you can pivot on the role to see the aggregate
amount and degree of change each role will experience. This is a simple
process, but the result is powerful and informative in many ways. First,
you will have created an inventory of change by process and role (always
start with a documented list!). Second, you will see that not everyone is
impacted by the change to the same degree. Being able to articulate who
will be impacted and to what level is very illuminating, especially when
you are planning your OCM approach and leader focus. This process
also addresses resistance to the change.

2) Case for Change and Vision for Future

The first question people typically ask when a change is introduced is,
"Why?" They want to understand first and foremost why the change is
good for the organization. Once they do, their next question is, "Why is
it good for me?" The first answer needs to be articulated by the highest-
ranking leader possible—no one lower in the org chart than the project

sponsor. The explanation of the need for the project is called a Case for Change and it should capture the key circumstances and implications of the current-state challenges, as well as a rationale for why staying with the status quo is not acceptable. The sponsor's second task is to lay out the *Vision for Future*, which will set forth the target end state and the rationale of why the suggested change is preferable to the alternatives (or to doing nothing).

Once the Case and Vision have been articulated, they need to be repeated. And repeated. And repeated. From the leader who first articulated the Case and Vision on down to the managers of the impacted individuals, the story needs to be consistent. Failure to have a consistent Case and Vision will raise doubts in the minds of the very people who need to accept that the change is good for the organization.

The fidelity and effectiveness of the Case and Vision can be measured both quantitatively and qualitatively, which means they can be reported upon to ensure the story is landing within the organization. If they are not landing with the target audiences as intended, more leader and sponsor attention is required to understand why. If it isn't landing anywhere, there's either a problem with the story or with consistency in how leaders are telling the story.

The articulation and acceptance of Case and Vision are necessary to enable the second part of change dialogue, and that is setting the context for change from the perspective of the individual. For effective change to occur, individuals need to accept that the change is good for the organization and for *them*. And the only way this can happen is if their manager takes the time to have a conversation with them about the details and context of the change.

That conversation can be laid out as following:

- Ask the employee what he/she thinks about the reason for change and the vision of the future state. If the employee has questions, answer them. If he/she doesn't think it's good for the organization, ask why. If the employee does think it's good, go to the next step.

• Share with the employee how the change will impact his/her role (provide the context for change), share the timetable for change, and then ask if he/she understands the change and thinks it will be good for his/her role. If there are questions, answer them. If the employee doesn't think it's good for him/her, ask why.

At this point, it will be clear if the employee is an advocate, neutral, or resistant to the change. This information can be tracked across the organization to provide metrics for adoption over the course of the initiative. At the very least, it will inform how much acceptance and resistance to the change exists in the organization.

3) Resistance Management

Project managers will be very familiar with this process, since Resistance Management follows the same approach as Risk Management, with the key difference being that Resistance Management focuses on the human risks to success. Identifying resistance to change will occur throughout a project, and assessing and executing the appropriate responses to that resistance follows the same framework of Risk Management. The important distinction is that you need to ask specific questions about, and look for specific evidence of, human resistance to the change.

When I perform the Change Management role on projects, these assessments are the first things I guide clients to focus on, with the addition of a stakeholder assessment. That stakeholder assessment is very similar to the stakeholder management approach within the Project

Management discipline, with the possible difference that in this case you want to identify what the stakeholder's disposition toward the change is and whether they are skilled in leading change. These two factors will inform whether additional coaching or sponsor engagement is required for your OCM plan.

HOW OCM BENEFITS FROM PROJECT MANAGEMENT

Combining OCM and Project Management is just like the old Reese's Peanut Butter Cup slogan: "Two great tastes that taste great together." It's a symbiotic relationship—OCM initiatives are more likely to succeed when Project Management best practices are applied (but that should be no surprise to you, right?).

As an example, another project success factor that should be applied to OCM initiatives is minimizing scope and requirements, as we should challenge and reduce the amount of change occurring in the end product in order to make it more consumable. The paradox in reducing the amount of change for users, however, is that it usually requires more change on the part of leaders. Both need to exist in order for both to succeed. And if only 30% of OCM efforts are successful, as some studies suggest is the case with projects, then both would benefit from the use of Project Success Checklists, right?

ORGANIZATIONAL CHANGE MANAGEMENT: CONCLUSION

I have never been a fan of measuring project success solely by whether a team has delivered on time and on budget. Attainment of the targeted objectives, achieving user adoption, and happy stakeholders—these seem like more crucial factors to success. That's why I believe the project manager of the future will evolve beyond scope, schedule, and budget to include a fourth focus: adoption.

In this vision, the project manager of the future is not responsible for performing the role of the change manager on the project, just as the project manager is not responsible for writing software, attaching the wing to the fuselage, or swinging a hammer. However, the project manager *is* responsible for scheduling the work, assigning the work, and making sure the work gets done—and that includes ensuring adoption. The greater the level of adoption, after all, the greater the odds that the project will achieve its target ROI.

Of course, one could argue that adoption is included in scope; I'll be good with that argument once I start seeing scope documents articulate the approach and measurements for adoption. Until then, I'm a fan of the *Four Horsemen of the Success-ocalypse*: Scope, Schedule, Budget, and Adoption.

KEY POINTS FOR CHAPTER 14:

- Project Management and OCM are equally important to project success; the principles within both are proven to drive better results.

- Applying a formal OCM methodology has shown to make projects six times more likely to deliver desired project results than those projects that do not apply an OCM approach.

- By performing three principles of OCM on projects—developing a compelling Case for Change that aligns organizational drivers and project goals; performing a Change Impact Analysis to identify what is changing, who will be impacted by the change, and to what degree they will be impacted; and performing Resistance Management by identifying where people will resist the change being introduced and determining proactive ways to address the resistance—

you will be better able to identify the scope required to increase acceptance, engagement, and adoption by your target audience.

- The project manager of the future will focus on adoption just as much as they focus on scope, schedule, and budget in order to manage and deliver on both sides of the ROI equation.

SECTION 3

Making Your Own Project

Success Checklist

CHAPTER 15

DIY Checklist: How to Create and Use a Project Success Checklist

Charity starts at home, as the saying goes, and given those abysmal-to-mediocre project success rate statistics I've already shared, I know I'm open to receiving any help and luck I can get. That's why I am grateful for having been present for Jim Johnson's keynote address about the top ten reasons projects succeed. I'm also thankful I realized that the strength of the Project Success Checklist is in the creation, collaboration on, and implementation of success factors to increase the likelihood of project success. By developing a Do-It-Yourself (DIY) checklist process, I am assured of having a highly-relevant and tailored list of success factors custom-built for my project by those who are most familiar with the work and challenges ahead.

Now that you have seen the factors on my list, let's talk about the specific steps for how to create your own Project Success Checklist and how to effectively use it on your projects.

HOW TO CREATE YOUR PROJECT SUCCESS CHECKLIST

Just as I took Mr. Johnson's list and personalized it to work for me, here is the process I recommend for creating your own Project Success Checklist. A similar version of this process can also be used when facilitating the creation of a checklist with stakeholders.

1) Identify Success & Failure Factors

I've already given you two Project Success Checklists, Mr. Johnson's version and my modified version—so start with those as you begin to build your own. If you played along with the 73-second activity in Chapter 1, you will have already identified a few. Take this to the next level by creating two columns on a sheet of paper or in a document on your computer. Label one column "Success Factors" and the other column "Contributors to Failure," and then start your own brainstorming session by identifying all the factors that have contributed to project successes or failures in your own experience.

In doing this exercise, think back on all those projects you've worked on that have met their objectives, and see if you can identify some of the factors that contributed to those projects being successful. Next, think about the challenges those projects had to overcome, and identify the main factors that helped you to overcome them. All projects, successful or not, have to overcome challenges, and there's likely a direct correlation between the efforts applied to overcome the challenges and the success of each project. Add those contributing factors to your "Success Factors" column.

Next—and sorry, I know this can be painful—go ahead and recall those projects that did not successfully met their objectives, and specifically think about the challenges that knocked the project sideways. Also, think about *when* those challenged projects were knocked off track and identify any root causes for their eventual failure. Now add that information to your "Contributors to Failure" column.

2) Group the Factors

Once you have exhausted your list of contributing success and failure factors, group the factors that are similar so that each listed factor is a unique factor. Some of the failure factors will be the opposite of your success factors (e.g., "Lack of visible and aware executive sponsorship" is akin to "effective sponsorship"), so those are easy to group. If any of the factors appear to be value-positive or value-negative—for instance, "great communication" or "bad coworker hygiene," I suggest making the factor value-neutral by removing the qualifier. For example, "coworker hygiene" is just as informative without the qualifier—and the main point is to focus and monitor the presence and positive application of the factor on the project ("hygiene," in this case) to help increase its likelihood of success (NOTE: I hope you never have to list "coworker hygiene" as a success factor on any of your projects).

The next thing is to cross off any factors that could be considered "table stakes," or prerequisites, for general workplace functionality—coworker hygiene, trust, or communication, for example. The hygiene factor should be a general condition of employment, so it's easy to remove that one; factors such as trust and communication, meanwhile, are so broad that they almost lose their meaning.

After I have my audiences write down their success factors and then ask them to share what they've written, typically both "trust" and "communication" are offered up. Now, don't get me wrong—both are extremely important behaviors that contribute to success. But without a more granularly defined factor, I don't know how to validate and measure the presence or contribution of either one. Yes, good communication can lead to clearer understanding of project objectives and task assignments, as well as the identification and resolution of problems, but those are three very specific contributing factors in their own right (and they are much more informative and easier to measure). I'd much rather have those three factors than the singular "good communication" on my list. Furthermore, the PricewaterhouseCoopers 2012 study I cited in Chapter 1 actually found an inverse correlation between good project communication and staying on schedule and on budget—those projects with good communication had lower rates of on-schedule and on-budget delivery.[63] I'm not sure what that means exactly, but it sounds a little like a backhanded compliment. "You have great communication for a project that doesn't deliver well."

Trust, meanwhile, is awesome when it's present on projects—but I think we've all worked on projects where there was little, if any, trust, and yet those projects still successfully attained their objectives. So while trust is an accelerator for getting work done, and while it does reduce costs and problems,[64] it doesn't seem to be a top ten contributing factor to success. Now, if this was a checklist for building strong teams, trust will absolutely be on the list. Instead, this checklist is about getting stuff done, and it's important to know the difference.

3) Rank the Factors

Now it's time to rank the factors you've listed by their contribution to project success—based on your experience, of course. Do a second pass through on your list by comparing each factor to the factors above and below on the list. Remember, all factors will contribute to success on some level; some factors will contribute more than others, but it's the successful application and achievement of *all* factors that will increase your likelihood of success.

Some people have asked me why the checklist needs to be prioritized. I used to think it didn't matter; all the factors on the list are key contributors to success. After all, it's the combined goodness of the whole that increases the likelihood of success. My mind was changed, however, when I was on a project where we were discussing success factors and someone asked what we would do if we found ourselves constrained due

---

63. PricewaterhouseCoopers 2012 Insights and Trends: Current Portfolio, Programme, and Project Management Practices, pg. 4. Haven't wrapped my head around this one either.

64. Stephen M. R. Covey's *Speed of Trust* provides his argument for trust as the following equation: "When trust is up, speed goes up and costs go down. When trust is down, speed goes down and costs go up." Page 13.

to limited time and resources—in other words, if we were forced to pick one factor over another, which one would we pick? If we had an issue that required attention in both the executive sponsorship and skilled resources areas, but we could only address one issue at the time, which one would we focus on? In this case, the answer for the team was executive sponsorship, which by extension meant that executive sponsorship had a higher priority listing than skilled resources. The conversation about prioritization is very illuminating in itself, and on the rare occasions when you have to choose between two factors, knowing ahead of time which factors are identified as higher priorities will inform that decision.

4) Finalize the List (sort of)

Once you have settled on your top ten factors (or eleven factors—who's to say which is best?), you'll want to get out your chisel and start etching the list into stone.

Wait a minute—not only is that a few millennia off from being good advice (you thought you hated doing documentation now, right?), the list is not complete. Nor will it ever be. As your experience grows and you take on different projects—and as you collaborate with sponsors and stakeholders on your projects—your list may evolve to meet ever-changing identified needs. I don't recommend chiseling anything into stone, whether actually or metaphorically; rather, I suggest you accept that your list will change, and look toward improving it as situations demand.

5) Create a Cheat Sheet

Your list of factors can be powerful by itself, but I recommend taking it a couple of steps further and creating a smart "cheat sheet" that will help you facilitate good conversations with sponsors and stakeholders about how to apply the contributing factors.

The first step in creating your one-page cheat sheet is to identify questions that will help you determine whether each factor is being implemented correctly on the project. For instance, for the success factor "minimize scope and requirements," an appropriate question that validates the factor is in place is, "Do we need everything we have listed for scope?" In this situation, the second or third answer will likely be more informative than the first, because the first will typically be a knee-jerk, "Of course we do" response. My counsel is to count to ten, enjoy the silence, and hope someone else offers up the first sacrificial piece of scope after thinking about the question for a moment. A good example of that second response might be, "Well, I'm not sure about that. Don't get me wrong, I think the 'Scratch and Sniff' requirement is really cool, but I'm not sure it's necessary for a successful spreadsheet application." By writing down a few probing questions for each of the success factors, you will create a "cheat sheet" that will remind you of the right things to ask to ensure the proper application of all of your success factors.

The second step for creating the "cheat sheet" version is to make a short list of simple actions for implementing each factor. In the above "minimize scope and requirements" case, for instance, a way to implement the factor can be to hold a "Do we need everything we have?" meeting with stakeholders. Kicking off that meeting, you can announce, "For each piece of scope, we need to determine whether that scope is a value add to attaining the project objectives or if it's required in order to attain our project objectives." By setting this goal, you will force a discussion about what is truly necessary to achieve the project objectives and what the "nice to have" items are—by the end of meeting you will hopefully have eliminated any work that's not going to drive value or help you achieve your project objectives.

Once you have your list of contributing factors, probing questions to ask, and simple steps to implement, I recommend that you squeeze all that content into one page. Here is what my Project Success Checklist looks like:

Success Factor	Questions	Action
1. Employee Involvement	How are we collecting requirements? How do we know we're satisfying a need?	Engage the end-users to develop requirements and test prototypes. Articulate the user story.
2. Executive Sponsorship	How engaged is the executive sponsor? How high in org can you go for escalation point?	Identify your project champion and engage to ensure continuous support
3. Clear Business Objectives	How many words does it take to describe goals? Do stakeholders articulate the goals the same way?	Create criteria for articulating business objectives and ensuring expectation-delivery alignment
4. Stakeholder Engagement	Have the stakeholders been identified? Do Stakeholder Management & Adoption Plans exist?	Identify all stakeholders and communication requirements, execute to plan to foster support

(continued on next page) ▶

Success Factor	Questions	Action
5. Project Leadership	Are team members being told what to do or are they inspired to accomplish their work?	Be intentional about employing principles of leadership to improve your ability to accurately set, manage, and define expectations
6. Minimize Scope & Requirements	Do we *have* everything we *need*? Do we *need* everything we *have*?	Identify steps to reduce scope, adopt iteration approaches, and frequently deliver and measure against goals
7. Proactive Risk Management	Are we continuously identifying new risks and monitoring risk triggers?	Routinely review risks response plans and discuss new and changing risks.
8. Take Corrective Action	When a significant issues occurs, is the Project Manager actively orchestrating the analysis and response?	Identify a mentoring for the Project Manager to review and audit performance and provide guidance.

▶

Success Factor	Questions	Action
9. Fostering Joint Accountability	How is accountability defined on the project? Do team members hold each other accountable?	As a team, define accountability and ground rules for expectations for holding each other accountable.
10. Skilled Resources	Do we have the right resource skill sets to deliver on business needs?	Perform internal capability assessment to determine alignment with Strategic resource needs
11. Org Change Management	What preparations have been made to engage end-users in the solution that will increase adoption?	Identify the change the solution creates and select methods to help end-users engage in and accept the change.

As you see, not a lot of room for detail, but this one-pager is easy enough to carry around, pin to your cube wall, and share electronically with others. If you deem that any additional detail is required, you can create a separate, longer document where you flesh out the information by listing more questions and more steps. I have found that this one-pager is sufficient to start the dialogue. Speaking of which—let's talk about how to talk about the Project Success Checklist conversation with our colleagues, sponsors, and stakeholders.

HOW TO USE THE PROJECT SUCCESS CHECK-LIST WITH SPONSORS & STAKEHOLDERS

While the original creation of your Project Success Checklist may be a solo activity, you can derive a lot more value from the list if you use it as a team sport. You can think of this as "crowdsourcing"—a new term for surveying a population and going with their collective genius. My favorite example of crowdsourcing comes from a 2012 TED presentation by Lior Zoref called "Of Oxes and the Wisdom of Crowds,"[65] where he brought a live ox onto the stage and asked attendees to guess the weight of the animal by sending a text message with their estimate. The 500 submitted responses ranged from 300 to 8,000 lbs; the average of the responses was 1,792. The actual weight of the ox was 1,795—just three pounds above the average of responses. Mind blown, right?

Since the Project Success Checklist is based on best practices, and since crowdsourcing is an effective way of collecting best practices (no bull, ox!), our next step after creating our list is to crowdsource the checklist to make sure you've captured the correct success factors. Crowdsourcing the Project Success Checklist with your colleagues is a great way to help validate the factors you've already identified, and is potentially a great way to also identify factors you have not yet contemplated. Crowdsourcing has the additional value of you bringing the concept of a Project Success Checklist to your colleagues, which will in turn help them better plan and manage their projects. Kudos for you. But the most direct impact crowdsourcing the checklist will have upon your projects will come from engaging your sponsors and key stakeholders in a dialogue about the factors that will drive success.

One of the first discussions you have with your sponsor should be about how they will define success for the project. A smart follow-up question would be to ask the sponsor what are or will be contribut-

---

65. I would have loved to have seen Lior Zoref's TED Talk—hopefully TED will publish the video one day. For now, you can read about it here: http://blog.ted.com/2012/02/29/of-oxes-and-the-wisdom-of-crowds-lior-zoref-at-ted2012

ing factors to success. After your sponsor has responded, bring forward your checklist, explain that you created it based on your experience leading projects, and humbly suggest that you both walk through the list to validate and modify as you both see fit for the project at hand.

In my experience, sponsors are looking for the project manager to bring their skills and experience, an informed point of view on how to lead and manage projects, and recommendations for how to improve planning and managing of the project. By facilitating the dialogue about project success factors, you will increase your sponsor's level of confidence and trust in your abilities to focus on the right things. Once you have engaged the sponsor in a dialogue about success factors, you are ready to engage the key stakeholders in a similar conversation. This can be performed individually or as a group—regardless, the goal is to create a documented list of success factors that the entire project leadership agrees to as being the most important contributing factors to a successful project.

"Why would a documented list of project success factors be an important thing to agree upon?" you ask. Because if implemented correctly, you can use this agreed-upon list to perform many Project Management tasks, including:

- Planning the Project

- Making Project Decisions

- Performing Risk Identification

- Assessing Project Health

- Facilitating Project Problem Solving

- Conducting Project Lessons Learned

"What if the project stakeholders or team members resist by saying that their expertise cannot be replaced by a checklist?" you ask. I would remind them that checklists are not meant to replace expertise, but instead provide reminders on process and proper procedures to ensure our expertise is well-spent on the important stuff. According to Dr. Atul Gawande, the best checklists are "not comprehensive, how-to guides. They are quick and simple tools aimed to buttress the skills of expert professionals." [66] You apply the expertise for the difficult tasks, the checklist reminds you to do the simple stuff that has dire consequences if forgotten.

Now, let's go through each one of those activities and I'll share how I've used the Project Success Checklist with sponsors and key stakeholders to improve our odds of achieving project success.

1) Planning the Project

In the very act of sharing the Project Success Checklist with your sponsor and key stakeholders at the beginning of the project and soliciting their input about what the right factors to focus on for this project, you are including the checklist factors in the planning process. This, in turn, gets sponsor and stakeholder engagement and alignment on incorporating those success factors into the project plan—which both makes you look smart and boosts the sponsor and stakeholders' trust and confidence in your abilities. Build a better plan and look good, too—what a bonus!

When you start to build out the details of your project plan, make sure that within the plan, all the factors are represented by deliverables and tasks. Here are some ideas for how to do that, using my first three factors on a software development project as the example:

- **User Involvement**

  - *Requirements Planning*—Interview a representative group of target users to understand current process

---

66. *The Checklist Manifesto*, Dr. Atul Gawande, pg. 128

and pain points, collect their ideas on how to improve processes and software tools, and discuss with the team how to incorporate those items into the product design.

☐ **Prototyping**—Review the prototype with a representative group of users to get their feedback. Compare the prototype with initial feedback collected during requirements planning, and validate if the prototype meets their needs based on feedback. Share the users' feedback with your team for further contemplation and design modification.

☐ **Functional Review**—As functional requirements are developed, review them with representative users to demonstrate the functions and collect feedback. Incorporate the feedback into the functional requirements and product design.

☐ **User Acceptance Testing**—Engage representative users in acceptance testing of the new tool; assess their feedback and determine if changes are necessary.
Training—Establish a representative group of users to learn the new tool so they will be able to lead training for their colleagues.

● **Executive Sponsorship**

☐ **Regular Status Reports**—Develop a cadence for providing updates on project progress and issues, giving awareness of potential risks and recommending specific actions for the sponsor to perform on behalf of the project.

❒ *Escalation Path*—Develop and review a document that highlights the process to be followed when sponsor intervention is required.

❒ *Sponsor Demos*—Schedule functional demonstrations of the tool with the sponsor to demonstrate your progress; at the demos, share user feedback and next steps and collect feedback from your sponsor, then make modifications as necessary.

● **Clear Business Objectives**

❒ Chartering—Obtain sponsor and key stakeholder agreement on the project Problem Statement, Business Objectives, and Acceptance Criteria.

❒ Scoping—Align all scope items with your Business Objectives and assign them priority levels.

❒ Requirements—Align all requirements with your Business Objectives and assign priority levels; develop measurement mechanisms to validate them upon completion.

❒ Acceptance Criteria—Measure and validate that Business Objectives have been delivered upon.

Earlier, I mentioned the Project Management mantra: "Plan the work, work the plan." In the case of the Project Success Checklist, one could say, "Plan the check(list), check the plan"—it might not be as catchy, but hopefully it does make it clear that you can easily create tasks based on your checklist to ensure the factors are baked into your plan. In doing so, you are planning for success—and planning for success is part of what makes success happen.

2) *Making Project Decisions*

The reason "Clear Business Objectives" is #3 on my Project Success Checklist is, as I stated before, because these objectives should be the basis of all project decisions. For example, you might be faced with decisions such as:

- *"Should our building requirements include a 10,000-square-foot auditorium, or shall we rent space when needed?"*

- *"Do we increase our budget and hire two more contractors, or do we delay our launch by a month?"*

- *"Our launch date is really important, but I think we might not have a valuable solution if we leave this feature out; can we add it without increasing our schedule risks?"*

The business objectives for a project should be clearly stated at the beginning, because they will provide guidance for the vast majority of business decisions you make during the project. The same goes with the Project Success Checklist, and this is the main reason to prioritize the list.

During the project, there may come a time when you will be faced with a decision between two of the success factors. Of course, optimally, you will be able to embed all factors at all times, and you should plan and continually strive for this. However, as projects often become challenged at some point, you may have to make a decision or recommendation that puts two success factors at odds. This is where prioritization and alignment with the project business objectives will be your guide.

3) *Performing Risk Identification*

Clearly, the checklist highlights those factors that drive project success, but there's a dark underbelly as well: all of the items on your Project Success Checklist have inverse risks associated with them, making your success factors a great place to start when conducting Risk Identification. Here are a few examples of what I mean:

Success Factor	Inverse Risks of Factor
#6—Minimize Scope & Requirements	• Incorrect prioritization or removal of requirement may reduce overall value of end product • Late identification of previously deprioritized scope as crucial step in build process may force a significant delay in schedule
#7—Proactive Risk Management	• Heightened awareness of risks may cause a high level of stakeholders angst, resulting in pressure to prioritize all risks at the same level • Lack of proper risk management may impact budget and schedule
#8—Taking Corrective Action	• Sponsor/stakeholder pushback on formal problem-solving process during moments of crisis may result in inefficient and ineffective problem-solving • Involving too many stakeholders in the problem-solving process may equate to not being able to obtain agreement on a solution

As you can see, the Project Success Checklist serves as an informative, through-the-looking-glass tool—one that allows you to identify the inverse potentiality if any of your success factors are not in play.

4) Assessing Project Health

The Project Success Checklist is a great assessment and diagnostic tool for determining how projects are doing, too. Whether your Project Management colleagues are asking you to assess their project, or you're managing other project managers and are in need of a good performance assessment tool, you can use your checklist to evaluate the situation. When you use your list, you will easily come up with questions like:

- "Tell me how the project has involved users in the planning, design, and testing of the product?" (#1—End User Involvement)

- "Tell me how your executive sponsor is engaged in the project?" (#2—Executive Sponsorship)

- "If I were to ask the key stakeholders—or anyone on the project team—would they be able to tell me what the top three objectives are for the project? And if yes, what evidence do you have that points to them being able to recite those top three objectives?" (#3—Clear Business Objectives)

I have also used the Project Success Checklist to assess project health for clients—sometimes in response to being asked, and sometimes proactively, when my intention was to *speak with evidence* when sharing concerns about the health of a project. The checklist is a great way to frame the conversation and allow clients to assess the project themselves using the factors as criteria; once that's done, you can discuss possible remedies.

The use of the Project Success Checklist as a *health check assessment tool* came from my colleague, Colin Smith, who approached me after attending one of my workshops and shared that he had used my checklist to assess the health of his client's project. He opened his laptop and showed me a form that had the success factors in the left column, a Red-Yellow-Green status indicator in the middle column, and data and evidence to support the status indicator in the right column. I was already pretty proud of my Project Success Checklist, but now my colleague had just extended the asset into an even more powerful tool (tip of the hat to Colin!), and it made me even prouder. I have now used the checklist several times as a project health check tool, each time with great results.

5) Facilitating Project Problem Solving

One of my favorite approaches to problem-solving is the Five Whys. The concept is simple: when attempting to find the root cause of a problem, you first ask a "why" question—for instance, "Why is the delivery of goods late?"—and then proceed to ask another "why" question based on the response:

Responese:	"Because Fulfillment shipped it late."
Why #2	"Why did they ship it late?"
Response:	"Well, they actually hit their 1-day service level agreement; the problem was that they received the order late."
Why #3	"Why did Fulfillment receive the order late?"
Response:	"Order Processing received the order on Friday, and they didn't send the order to Fulfillment until Monday."
Why #4	"Okay, why did Order Processing receive the order on Friday when the order was due to be received here on Thursday?"
Response:	"Procurement placed the order on Friday."
Why #5	"Why did Procurement place the order on Friday?"
Response:	"We didn't tell Procurement when we needed the goods to be received."

Now, "five" is a merely a suggestion for how many "why" questions to ask, but heuristics show that it usually takes five to get to the root cause. Of course, our responder in the above case could have offered the last line as their first response, saving four whys. However, as you can see in the above example, if you stop at any of the responses to Whys #1–4 and attempt to fix the "problem" there, you will only be address-ing *symptoms* of the problem, not the problem itself, which is that your team didn't tell Procurement when they needed the goods.

I've heard this tool was developed by Sakichi Toyoda, back when Toyota Industries was creating what is now known as Lean process development—I would wager, however, that the credit actually be-longs to one of Sakichi's children. How this plays out in my head is that Sakichi was at home one night after a long day of process re-engineering when he told his kid (who, I'm assuming, was a two- or three-year-old), that it was bedtime. And like all good two- and three-year-olds around the world, his kid was really into problem-solving and wanted to understand the root cause of this decision. So Sakichi probably lost his patience at about round five of "why" and finally responded with, "Because I'm your father and I told you so." With that, little Toyoda went off to bed—and a great problem-solving tool was born.

How does this relate to project problem-solving and the Project Success Checklist? In the course of problem-solving and implementing the Five Whys, you want to be keenly aware (i.e., hyper-vigilant), about any problems and/or root causes that are directly related to your success factors. Clearly, if the problem you're facing is created by or affects a success factor, the priority of that problem just jumped to code red and requires your immediate attention. If this occurs, it should trigger you to review Chapter 11 on Taking Corrective Action.

6) Conducting Project Lessons Learned

In the next chapter, I'll share a story about how I once used the Project Success Checklist for the basis of a Lessons Learned session, but I want to give you a condensed version here of what I learned from that experience:

- Hold the Lessons Learned session after each major phase instead of waiting until the end of the project.

  - ⌐ At the end of the project, people may have forgotten the details from earlier phases or would rather let sleeping dogs lie and not bring up "old news," so they'll focus only on the most recent issues.

  - ⌐ Most of the recent problems will likely be the result of work performed (or *not* performed) earlier in the project. So the recent challenges may be a symptom disguised as a root cause.

  - ⌐ All benefits identified at a session held at the end of a project will not be realized on the project they came from. Great for the next project manager; bummer for you.

- Honor the past. Whatever form this takes, the important thing is to acknowledge that decisions are made based on the judgment and data available at the time. Hindsight is great—however, if used inappropriately, it can also make you look like a real jerk, and in many organizations, failing to respect previous decisions can land you in a bad position with stakeholders and team members.

● Using the "Continue Doing–Stop Doing–Start Doing" format allows your team to identify the things they should continue to do, the actions that should be eliminated in the future, and the things they should start doing that they have not yet tried. This is a slight add to the Plus/Delta format, where participants identify what's working well and what is not; the Continue–Stop–Start format focuses a little more clearly on the actions that need to be taken, so it feels more productive—and more proactive.

To integrate the Project Success Checklist into the Lessons Learned discussion, you can ask specific questions about each item—for instance:

● "We identified Key Stakeholder Engagement as a key factor for a successful project. What should we continue, stop, or start doing to better set and manage stakeholder expectations on this project?"

● "We developed a rigorous Risk Management plan for the project to identify and handle risks. What should we continue, stop, or start doing that would enable us to better manage risks on this project?"

● "In the beginning of the project, we said we needed to pay attention to Organizational Change Management in order to increase acceptance and adoption of our new solution. What are we doing that is working today, what are we doing that is not working, and what should we try doing to increase acceptance and adoption?"

By understanding and coming to agreement with your sponsor and key stakeholders on the most important contributing factors for success, you as the project manager will be able to lead all of the above activities with confidence that you know exactly what your project leadership demands of you. If your project objectives are your true north, then the Project Success Checklist can be your compass.

DIY CHECKLIST: CONCLUSION

As I shared earlier, the Project Success Checklist did not become valuable for me until I made it my own by identifying the factors that have contributed to success and failure *in my own experience.* Jim Johnson's Top Ten Reasons Projects Succeed list was a great start, but since three of the factors did not apply to my circumstances, for me it was incomplete. So I replaced those three with another three. And over the years, I have frequently reviewed and occasionally updated the list based on my experience and tailored it to the projects I'm working on.

The process for creating your own Project Success Checklist is simple: You can start with my checklist as a template, and then add to it by identifying the factors that have contributed to success and failure on your own projects, grouping similar factors, removing the duplicates, and then prioritizing the list down to a reasonable number. Then—and this is possibly the most important step—don't just save the list on your hard drive or in your desk drawer; instead, breathe life into it by sharing it with other project managers and getting their feedback. Share with them how to create their own lists—or, even better yet, collaborate with your Project Management team to create a list for all-around better performance.

By creating and sharing your Project Success Checklist with stakeholders, you have identified and incorporated those factors into your project plan, so success is guaranteed, right?

Simply stated, no. As I mentioned before, the presence of a checklist does not guarantee success. The checklist in the operating room does not guarantee that there will be no post-op complications. The checklist in the cockpit does not guarantee that there won't be unexpected issues for pilots to handle. And a Project Success Checklist does not guarantee that a project will attain its objectives. Project success is a combination of the sponsors and stakeholders, the team, and you, all contributing by performing your roles and tasks in an a synchronized attempt to deliver a product or solution that produces value for the organization; the Project Success Checklist is just a list of reminders of the contributing factors that will increase your likelihood of success in your endeavors.

KEY POINTS FOR CHAPTER 15:

- The Project Success Checklist becomes truly valuable when you make it your own by tailoring it to your projects, your environment, and your experiences. You *could* just use my checklist—however, making your own is invaluable. The ensuing conversations you'll have with colleagues, stakeholders, and sponsors as you go through this process will make for a better list, and will elevate their trust and confidence in your leadership capabilities.

- The Do It Yourself process ensures the critical success factors identified are relevant to your project and likely improves how you are perceived by your stakeholders for introducing the emphasis on planning for success.

- The process for creating your Project Success Checklist is very straightforward, and can even be a fun and informative exercise when performed with others. The last step of this process—creating the one-page "cheat sheet" version of your list—is the most visible form of the Project Success Checklist, since it's what will be proudly displayed on your cube or office wall (and of course you'll want to take it with you to every project meeting you attend, as well).

- Using the Project Success Checklist on your projects will ultimately generate the most value out of the whole experience. Not only can the checklist help you plan your projects, identify risks, and make project decisions, it can also be used as criteria for assessing project health and conducting Lessons Learned sessions. As you will read in the next chapter, there is very little value in merely creating a Project Success Checklist; you also have to prioritize the management of your project with it.

CHAPTER 16

Limitations of the Checklist:

The Path to Hell is Paved

with Good Intentions

f checklists are such valuable tools for focusing us on the keys to success, should we also create a checklist that helps us ensure the successful implementation of a Project Success Checklist?

Seems redundant, right? A checklist that ensures the successful implementation of a checklist begins to sound like an enigma wrapped in a conundrum trapped in a puzzle (would you have M.C. Escher[67] diagram the process flow for doing this?). Until a couple years ago, I would have laughed at the irony of the idea. And then, well, something happened and I started a checklist for implementing the Project Success Checklist. So far I only have one factor on it. But before I share that list, let me tell you about the time I made chocolate chip taquitos.[68]

IGNORANCE IS NOT ALWAYS BLISS

I wanted to thank a friend for doing something nice for me, so I decided to make them a dozen chocolate chip cookies. I printed a recipe from

---

67. For more on M.C. Escher: http://en.wikipedia.org/wiki/M._C._Escher
68. A taquito is a fried rolled tortilla with meat filling. Good finger food, loved by children and adults alike.

a website and headed off to the kitchen. I followed the directions and mixed the ingredients. When everything was supposedly ready, I laid out six cookie dough dollops and placed the cookie sheet into the oven. Twelve minutes later I went to pull out my cookie sheet—and my dollops had baked into flat circles.

Befuddled, I reached for the recipe and mentally went through all the instructions, the ingredients, and the steps, and was left scratching my head. I turned to my lovely wife and asked her if she knew what I'd done wrong. The analysis was, of course, delayed by her laughter as she looked down at my chocolate chip flats. She started running down the list of ingredients:

Wife: "½ cup butter?"
Me: "Yes."
Wife: "1 cup sugar?"
Me: "Yes."
Wife: "1 egg?"
Me: "Yes!"
Wife: "1 and a half cups of flour?"
Me: "What?! Of course not, you're testing me. It said ½ cup flour."
Wife: "Found it. That's your issue. You are missing an extra cup of flour."

At this point, my sons had swooped in like seagulls and started to roll the flat, sticky messes into what resembled taquitos—and I must admit, they weren't bad. Still, they weren't necessarily going to say the "thank you" I intended for my friend.

Since I'm embracing my new definition for accountability and asking my two questions (*How did I contribute to the situation?* and *What can we do to move toward desired outcomes?*; see Chapter 8), it would be erroneous to blame the recipe for my mistake; even though my ego wanted me to blame the printer or some other malfunction, it was me who did not follow the instructions as written. The fact of the matter was, I had missed a step of the recipe—and while my kids appreciated my lack of reading comprehension, it meant I had to start all over again. I followed the recipe with precision the second time, and the next batch turned out pretty darn good. Thank you, recipe; sorry for doubting you before.

Just as the recipe was not to blame when I didn't follow it, a checklist is not to blame when it is not used correctly. Dr. Atul Gawande's *Checklist Manifesto* highlights the value of checklists in keeping smart people from doing dumb things, reminding us that it's often the simple things that we do over and over again—the things that feel so routine that we think we don't need a *silly* checklist to remember them—that we forget to do. In the operating room, in the cockpit, and in the kitchen, checklists have proven invaluable to preventing the simple mistake that can lead to a critical failure.

Can you imagine going to the trouble of creating a Project Success Checklist, or any checklist for that matter, and then, when it counted, choosing to *not* use that checklist? Of course not—that would just be silly, right? Common sense would demand that you follow the checklist. If only common sense were a more common practice.

TAKING THE "CHECK" OUT OF THE CHECKLIST

A few years ago, a project's leadership team approached me about facilitating the development of a Project Success Checklist for their project. Now, the first phase of their project was already 100% late, and had mounting technical problems that had delayed the end of the first phase, so the leadership team was looking to change things up by identifying and applying Lessons Learned. The Project Success Checklist, they told me, seemed just the thing to focus the team on those key factors that would help them to start making more traction against their goals.

I was flattered when they approached me, and optimistic about the opportunity to help, so I was eager to take them through the Project Success Checklist creation process I described in Chapter 15. We agreed to have me facilitate a workshop where the leadership team could collaborate on the factors that should be included on their Project Success Checklist.

At the beginning of the workshop, I asked the leadership team to identify those factors that lead to successful projects in three categories: People, Process, and Technology. Once they'd done that, I then asked them to identify the factors that contribute to project failures in the same categories, because I wanted to prompt thought about the various factors. At the end of the brainstorms, we had two substantial lists with more than fifty items—according to my subscribed process, we then grouped the items and removed the duplicates. At that point, three dozen factors remained. I was honestly impressed—there were no shortages of ideas for what contributed to success and failure on this team. I thought their willingness to fully participate was a great sign.

Since everyone loves top ten lists, we agreed we needed to weed the list down to ten items. I asked each leader to vote on the top five factors they believed were the most important factors, and we eliminated half of the items on the list, leaving us with eighteen items. Six of the items had received more than three votes, so I wrote them on a separate whiteboard and said that these would be in our draft top ten list. Then we focused on the remaining twelve, looking to see if there were any commonalities between them, and in fact there were. One team member identified "people engagement" as a category by combining "getting people ready for change," "think out of the box," and "define clear roles and responsibilities." Another team member combined "benefits realization," "cost measurement," and "team engagement measurement" and coined the factor "performance measurement." When we were done finding affinities between the remaining factors, we were left with a total of eleven factors. I guess the leadership team had not seen the movie *Spinal Tap*,[69] but they had clearly seen the television show *Survivor*, because they decided they wanted to vote one factor "off the island," and did so by eliminating one.

We then turned our focus to prioritizing the ten success factors. As mentioned before in Chapter 15, the process of prioritizing these factors is a great one to engage in with stakeholders because it can highlight some previously undiscovered or unknown expectations, predispositions, and perspectives. In this case, the conversation did not disappoint. A telling sign was when "strong partnership with vendors" went toe-to-toe with "requirements management" in the prioritization ring. Because the project relied heavily on vendors, "requirements management" suffered an early knockout in the early rounds and fell to #7, while "strong partnership with vendors" jumped to #2. This concerned me because ultimately that "partnership" should be based on successful understanding and the ability to fulfill requirements. When I raised that concern, I was told that having a strong relationship with all the vendors was more critical to success because it would ensure that requirements would be appropriately managed and executed—besides, they said, "requirements management" was still on the list (in other words, they were recognizing both factors as critical). I also reminded them that I had suggested removing broad statements about communication, and pointed out that "open and honest communications" had been placed on the list at #5. They wanted to keep it there. After voicing my two concerns, I accepted that this was the leadership's success list and not mine, and thus their Project Success Checklist had been created.

The list was sent out to the entire project team and made into the theme of the upcoming Lessons Learned session that the leadership team was hosting. The purpose of the Lessons Learned meeting was to

---

69. Obviously with a Top Ten List, I'm a David Letterman fan. I'm also a fan of Spinal Tap, which is why I've allowed my list to go to 11. Spinal Tap was a rock-mockumentary film that chronicles the rise and fall of a fictitious heavy metal hair band in the 1980s. In one scene, the guitarist explains that his amplifier goes to 11 because on other amplifiers, when you get to 10 and want to go one more, there isn't that option.

collect feedback from the more than 150-person team on how best to integrate the success factors into the project and identify what needed to change in order to turn the trajectory of the project around. Remember, at this point it was 100% over schedule and there was no definitive path for how the team would hit their first major milestone, so the Project Success Checklist was viewed as part of the recovery process the leadership team was willing to undertake.

The large Lessons Learned workshop began with the leadership team announcing the ten success factors and then engaging the entire team in discussions about the key actions that the project should continue doing, stop doing, and start doing per each success factor to achieve project objectives. Picture, if you can, a large, cafeteria-sized room with ten three-by-nine-foot pieces of paper taped to the walls, each one filled with colorful words capturing the feedback for each of the factors. That alone was an impressive sight. A tremendous number of ideas were generated during the session, and those sheets were proof that team members were really engaged in coming up with improvements for the project.

Next, everyone was asked to vote on the top three things they believed should be addressed within any of the success factors. We gave every individual three sticky dots, and had them go up and place them next to those ideas they felt most strongly about. When I looked at those 10 large sheets of paper, 30 categories, at least 200 ideas, and more than 450 sticky dots, I'm sure I was smiling as broadly as the owner of local office supply store did when the project leaders went in to buy the materials. I was hopeful that this event would be the thing that would turn the project around: the leaders would empower the team to address and resolve the issues that had prevented success thus far, and the newly minted success factors would lead the team to success.

Well, not so fast; this story does not have a happy ending. While the top thirty ideas coming out of the Lessons Learned session were assigned to five improvement teams, and those teams diligently performed root cause analysis and problem-solving exercises to determine how to address and resolve key issues, things got off track when, shortly after the Lessons Learned session, the leadership team became preoccupied with the project's mounting technical problems. They took their collective eye off the improvement efforts, and it showed: they stopped attending improvement team readouts and responding to e-mails; they stopped referring to the success factors in their communications to the team; and worst, they ignored the factors altogether in their daily management of the project.

As I mentioned before, one value of the Project Success Checklist is to use it as a project health assessment, and I did use this team's created success list to assess the project twice: once before the Lessons Learned session and once after. The last time I used it to assess the project's health, I found several concerning issues. The first success factor was "executive sponsorship," which highlighted the value of holding people accountable for the delivery of scope—and yet with each delay announced no one was held accountable, nor was there any significant analysis performed as to why the delay occurred or how it could be prevented in the future. The second factor, "strong partnership with vendors," was not evident at all—the vendors were raising concerns and offering recommendations to the leadership team but their words were falling on deaf ears. The third factor, "robust project methodology," was also being ignored, as evidenced by the lack of diligent analysis of the problems or the work necessary to address and fix the problems. Instead, after each delay, a new release date was immediately announced by leadership, with no explanation of the cause or true impact of the delay. The old project "methodology" was winning out over the promise of a "robust" methodology, and the team was beginning to settle back into their old habits. The excitement for the future faded quickly, almost before the ink on the success factor cards had finished drying.

The team's Project Success Checklist lingered in obscurity for almost one year, right up until it was dusted off during planning discussions for the next Lessons Learned session. In those twelve months, the executive sponsor and project sponsor had both left the company, and that first milestone had finally been achieved—300% later than originally promised. It took another six months of poor performance for the project to be canceled. Over two years in development, hundreds of employees and vendors involved, millions of dollars spent, and a huge blow to the morale of those impacted. It makes you wonder if all the right factors were identified on the Project Success Checklist, what's the value of the checklist if it doesn't prevent the opposite of those success factors from occurring?

In the final analysis, I believe the answer exists within Jim Johnson's Top Five Reasons Projects Fail list:

- *Ambition*—failure to understand project/product limitations

- *Arrogance*—failure to acknowledge what the team cannot produce

- *Ignorance*—failure to understand what the team can do

- **Fraudulence**—lying about team's capabilities

- *Abstinence*—not paying enough attention to the project to ensure its success

This team created a Project Success Checklist midflight because it felt like the right thing to do in the face of mounting problems. And while the checklist contained factors that could easily have contributed to success *if they had been implemented*, they were also the factors that contributed to failure when ignored. Surgeons have checklists for procedures, but when they don't follow the checklists, they are just as liable to make a mistake as if they didn't have the checklist in the first place. In this example, the Project Success Checklist did not help deliver results because those factors that could have contributed to success were at best misunderstood, and at worst ignored. So it is likely that the project would have experienced the same results regardless of when the Project Success Checklist was created. A checklist is simply a piece of paper that captures good intentions—and as the old tale tells, the path to hell is paved with good intentions. In the conference room, just like in the cockpit and operating room, if project leaders and project managers have checklists but don't use them or don't know how to apply the success factors contained on the list, they should not be surprised that the end result is the same as if they never created a checklist in the first place.

With this in mind, here is my new checklist for the success implementation of a Project Success Checklist:

1. When creating the checklist, also develop the reinforcing mechanisms to ensure the checklist is used frequently (i.e., don't create it if you're not going to develop opportunities to use it).

That's all I have so far; perhaps that will be the topic of my next book.

KEY POINTS FOR CHAPTER 16:

- If you do not follow the process or do not apply the success factors on the Project Success Checklist you have created, the mere presence of a checklist will not save the project from failure nor increase the likelihood of success. The checklist by itself is not valuable, the value comes from creating and using it.

● If you are asked to create a Project Success Checklist for a project team, take it one step forward and create reinforcement mechanisms to ensure the checklist will be adopted, will be used frequently, and will have the intended positive consequences.

Conclusion

"If you do not change direction, you may end up where you are heading."
—Lao Tzu

In writing this book, I have received the counsel of many colleagues and friends. One of the best pieces of advice I received was that I should define success for the book, and to do so in a way that identifies the good, the better, and the best results. For me, "good" success means getting the book published—so if you are reading this, I've certainly attained my first level of success. My "better" success equates to sharing this valuable techniques to a wider audience. My "best" success would be for readers to create their own Project Success Checklists and apply them on their projects with outstanding results. In order to know if I've achieved this, I earnestly ask you to contact me at www.Roger Kastner. com and let me know if you have questions, or about your experiences with creating and using your own Project Success Checklist.

By now, hopefully, you agree that the Project Success Checklist is both a useful and a necessary tool. As Dr. Atul Gawande shared with us in *The Checklist Manifesto*, the list is a proven, valuable tool for highly intelligent, highly trained professionals who are more likely to make a "dumb" mistake when performing routines than they are when attempting something difficult and challenging. For project managers looking to increase their odds of project success, the Project Success Checklist is a valuable tool—when it's used appropriately. When the success factors on the checklist are misunderstood or ignored, however, the list becomes an unfulfilled good intention—and the results can be dire.

What I ask of you is to make this list your own by following the process I outlined in Chapter 15. Go ahead and start with mine; tailor it based on your own experiences, then take it to the next level by sharing it with your sponsors and stakeholders and collaborating with them to create the right list of factors for your project. Once you've figured out how to embed those factors into your scope, use the Project Success Checklist as an input for planning the project, for identifying risks to the project, and for assessing performance to goals on the project. Furthermore, share it with your Project Management colleagues: it will help them increase the likelihoods of success, and it will allow you to collaborate to create a standard Project Success Checklist for the organization that can be used for all projects. In fact, I have followed this process myself during the time it has taken me to write this book.

Since I began writing this book, I have started and completed a few projects which have led me to alter my own base Project Success Checklist. I have replaced one factor on my checklist based on my experience on those projects, which is a good reminder that the checklist is meant to evolve and change based on the needs of the individual project, the sponsor and stakeholders, and the organizational environment in which the project exists. The change I made to the list? I replaced Skilled Resources with Desired Behaviors, as in the desired behaviors that illustrate the project is being used as intended, and the business objectives of the project will be achieved. I found that by identifying these desired behaviors you can leverage them to:

- inform how to train users,

- direct managers or marketing to reinforce those desired behaviors, and

- measure behaviors as leading indicators to determine if the solution will successfully meet the business objectives of the project.

In my recent experience, Desired Behaviors has been such a driver for project success that it eclipsed the admittedly more obvious Skilled Resources on my Project Success Checklist. And I'm sure the checklist will evolve again, and that's exactly what it's meant to do.

But remember, it won't matter what's on your list if you do not first actively participate in the definition of success for the project and for your role as project manager. Just as success needs to be explicitly defined for a project, it needs to be defined for the role of project manager.

My simple mantra for success is: define it, plan it, measure it, and celebrate it.

- **Define it**—define what success means for you and for the project

- **Plan it**—plan for how you and your project will achieve success

- **Measure it**—identify the metrics that will allow you to measure progress towards your definition for success, and be sure to take corrective action when you are knocked off track

- **Celebrate it**—be sure to honor your achievement when you attain success

Projects are like marathons: if you do not define, plan, and prepare appropriately, you will likely be walking funny afterwards and disappointed with the results if you are fortunate to even make it to the finish line. On the flip side, if you *do* define, plan, and prepare well and then execute on your goals, no amount of soreness or blisters will stop you from beaming from ear to ear and receiving congratulations and high-fives from peers and colleagues.

As I've said more than once in these chapters, I do not want my performance on projects to be assessed against objectives that are out of my control and do not fairly measure my contribution (yes, I'm talking to you, "on-schedule and on-budget" people). Instead of metrics that have a number of variables, inputs, and stakeholders impacting them, I would rather be evaluated by the two key factors I can control: commitment management and taking corrective action. I value commitment management because *my* ability to manage my commitments enables my sponsors and stakeholders to manage their own commitments with their management and colleagues. Additionally, my ability to take corrective action when my project is knocked sideways by some unforeseen force is paramount to achieving those project commitments I've staked my definition of success upon. If I'm not able to get the project back on track in a timely and effective way, I will likely fail to deliver on scope, schedule, and budget expectations. Furthermore, my ability to marshal my troops and facilitate the problem-solving process while taking corrective action will greatly impact how my sponsor, stakeholders, and team members perceive my value as a professional project leader. Because of this, I believe measuring commitment management and the ability to take corrective action is much more useful, accurate, and productive than measuring adherence to scope, schedule, and budget in evaluating a project manager's performance.

Whichever research you want to believe—whether projects achieve success an average of 30% or 70% of the time—I'm sure we can agree we need all the luck we can get in order to achieve success on our projects. And if the Project Success Checklist can increase our odds of success, why wouldn't you use it to tip the odds in your favor?

Now, Project Management might not be brain surgery, but we can still benefit from using the same practices brain surgeons use when working on projects. If a checklist can contribute to the success of a surgery, it can help project managers successfully navigate projects to completion. Same for the cockpit of an airplane, if the checklist is vital to ensure safe flight, it should also help make your projects fly right. Personally, I have found that the Project Success Checklist to be a powerful tool that helps me plan and prepare my projects, build stronger relationships with my sponsor, stakeholders, and teammates, and most importantly prevent me from making simple mistakes. If a checklist can help keep a wristwatch out of someone's belly and help land a plane safely, it can also help you with your projects—go create a Project Success Checklist and try it for yourself.

About the Author

ROGER KASTNER has twenty years of experience leading and coaching individuals, teams, and organizations in raising the caliber of their strategy and execution talents to achieve greater success. Roger is a Project Management and Organizational Effectiveness consultant, where he splits his time between client project delivery, designing and facilitating workshops for colleagues and clients, and writing about Project and Change Management. Roger is also a Lead Instructor in the Project Management program at the University of Washington where he teaches about Project Leadership and Communications.

Roger has a BA from the University of California, Santa Barbara, and currently lives in Seattle with his wife and two children where he enjoys running in the rain and coaching youth lacrosse.

To follow Roger, you can catch him at one of the following:

* Web: www.RogerKastner.com

* Twitter: @RogerKastner

* Linkedin: Roger Kastner

Acknowledgments

First and foremost, I want to thank my wife, Lara, for her love and support through this entire process. I could not have completed this book without her love. I want to thank my sons, Duncan and Ian, for being the protagonists in many of the stories I share in the book and in the classroom and for the daily inspiration they give me to be better at everything I do.

For their endearing encouragement and support, I want to thank my parents, Marge and Larry. Thank you to my brother, Tom, for all the jokes that didn't make it into the book.

For the numerous thought-provoking discussions that in many ways contributed to ideas within this book, I want to thank Chrissy Vonderach, Alissa Barnes, Kelli Hildebrand, Patrick Hildebrand, Dan Maycock, Colin Smith, and Kimberly Southern-Weber.

A huge thanks to my colleagues at Slalom Consulting who have supported my efforts in bringing this idea to the training room, the auditorium, the Slalom blog, and now to these pages: Tony Rojas, John Tobin, Brian Jacobsen, Clare Pedersen, Tricia Peterlin, Jila Javdani, Ray Pitts, Carl Manello, and David Row. Also thank you to Keith Newbern, Bruce Wilson, Annie Ezell-Cave, Darryl Price, Robert Barrantes, and Maggie Sheldon: I am grateful for your expert editing and guidance in helping me bring my words to the page.

Thanks also go to Brooke Warner and her team for her guidance during the editing and publishing final push. To everyone who participated in the crowdsourcing of the title for the book, thank you for your inspiration—*you were right!*

Lastly I want to thank my grandfather, Duncan Powers, who shared with me his passion for flight, taught me the harder choice in any decision is the right option, and to "straighten up and fly right." Hat's off to you, sir.

Index

CPSIA information can be obtained at www.ICGtesting.com
Printed in the USA
LVOW08s0309270115

424422LV00009B/31/P